How to Draw 60 Native California Plants and Animals

Written & Illustrated by Sama Wareh

Edited by Sarah Wareh

ISBN - 10: 1466367253
ISBN - 13: 978-1466367258

LCCN: 2012912120

Special Thanks:

To my parents, for teaching me from early on to love and respect nature.

To Sarah Wareh, my older sister, for her patience and unwavering support to make this book.

To Ronna Wareh, my oldest sister and spirited mountain woman, for taking me on my first real hike and teaching me to keep going, because the top of the mountain was worth it.

To Monica Edwards, for being my pillar of support.

To Bo Glover, for his endless dedication to environmental education.

To Leslie Helliwell, A.K.A. The Walking Encyclopedia, for spending countless hours reviewing this book.

&

To Lori Whalen, for her dedication to restoring California to its native landscape.

Dedication

I dedicate this book to Ahmad Wareh. Ahmad is my uncle from Syria who is no longer with us. He was a homeopathic healer and was able to communicate with birds and animals. He took no money in exchange for his services and spent his life creating a database of plants and their remedies. One memory I will never forget was a summer in Syria when a cyst in my eye was inflamed. It was quite painful and three different doctor visits did nothing for it. My uncle scolded me for not coming to him first. He boiled a few white sage leaves in water and then let the water cool down. He had me rinse my eye with the soothing white sage tea. The burning instantly ceased, and in that moment, I believed in natural healing and the power of plants. I had lived for years around white sage, playing tag with my friends in the dry coastal sage scrub in Mission Viejo, California. I never noticed how valuable my playground had been until I got into the environmental field after college, and it suddenly dawned on me: My uncle used a few of these California plants for remedies as did the Native Americans. I am forever grateful to my uncle for instilling a love and appreciation of nature in me and for passing on the torch of conservation, even if it originated from another country entirely— for ultimately, it is all one world that we share.

Contents

Intro

Isn't it true that the closer we observe something, whether it be animated or not, the more connected we feel to it? For instance, most people feel like they know certain celebrities although they probably never met them before in their life. The reason is because they have observed them on television, and in that sense they feel like they know them. Nature is the same way. The more we observe something, the more we feel like we are somehow connected to it.

The word conservation is derived from the Greek word "conservo" which means to keep or observe. It is difficult to conserve something if we don't value it or are even unaware of its existence.

This book is:

- *intended* to enhance awareness of the beauty and significance that our backyard in California possesses. What appears to be just some dried up brush on the side of a freeway is actually a coastal sage scrub medicine pantry. What appears to be just an ordinary lizard is the reason we have less Lyme disease in California. The more educated we become on the way nature functions in its natural form, the better we understand the ecological value in its preservation. It is my hope that whoever uses this book will get to know the very California plants and animals they learn to draw and find themselves excited to be able to point them out in real life.

- *designed* to photocopy, hand out to kids and adults, utilize for making journals and creating workshops, use as a tool to teach more about California animals and plants...

and, oh yes, to learn how to draw of course! When you draw something, you really have to look at it closely and break it apart. You have to observe the fine details and describe them in your head. By doing this, you will be able to identify it in the wild.

- a *compilation* of whatever I have in my head and know how to do. If I know how to make tea out of a plant, the instructions for it will be in the back. The "How to Draw" page will refer you to the index if there is more to learn about it. If there isn't more info, it just means to look up the rest on your own. There is a lot to learn about all plants and animals, and I am constantly boggled by how much more there is to learn every day.

- *formatted* in a unique manner. It was difficult to choose which reptiles, mammals, plants, arthropods, amphibians and birds to fit in this book, since California's diverse ecosystems is home to thousands of different, yet ecologically significant species. Furthermore, since this book is not just a drawing book but designed to teach about what is happening ecologically, I decided to place symbiotic or dependent species next to each other. This means you shouldn't be surprised if you open the bird section and find a plant. It just means that the plant means a lot to the bird..

If you have any questions, comments, or concerns, please visit www.warehart.com. I would love to hear from you!

Drawing Tips

"Everybody is a Genius. If you were to judge a fish based on its ability to climb a tree, it would think it were stupid."
– Albert Einstein

At some point in our lives while trying to pursue a goal, we were perhaps given the wrong tools to do it and, as a result, believed that we were incapable of achieving that goal. If somebody asked you to row a canoe with a fork, you might think you were really bad at it and would never try again. The worst thing that we can do is to give up on something, especially when that something—whatever it is—can be approached from a million different ways. Art is that way. There are hundreds of different ways to approach it. That's because art is ultimately about observing the world around us and documenting what we see, feel, or think in a visual way. There are a few techniques that can help when it comes to taking what we see and making it look real. These tips below are just guidelines to help the artistic process flow better.

1. Most of art is erasing, so prepare to erase. Translation: get hold of a decent eraser.

2. Try using a 6B pencil. (The lead is much softer and won't etch into your paper.)

3. Look at what you're drawing and make sure you have enough space on your paper to finish the drawing (i.e. don't start drawing a giraffe by placing the body in the middle of the page—you probably won't have enough space to make the neck long enough and will inevitably have to erase the entire body and move it towards the bottom of the page.

Relax. Art is about having *fun*. If you are not having fun, you are missing the point.

4. Start with basic shapes and try to break down complex shapes into smaller little shapes.

5. There will come a time in your drawing where you feel that it's not going the way you want it to go—push through that feeling, it's a sign you are very close. (Life is the same way.)

6. When trying to copy something, remember that 80% of your time should be spent observing it and describing what you see in terms of shapes and textures. By explaining it in your head, not only do you train your eye to draw what you actually see but you also carve it into your memory. This will help you remember how to draw that object later on, even if you aren't looking at it.

Example: If I were to draw a spider, I would say "The spider has two body parts; two touching ovals in the shape of the number eight. The bottom oval, three times the size of the top oval, is an upside down tear drop. On either side, there are four legs coming out of the center where the body parts meet. Two of the legs face up and two face down. There is hair (little lines) on the body of the spider and little hairs sticking out of the bottom of each leg of the spider."

"Architects cannot teach nature anything."
- Mark Twain

Reptiles &
Amphibians

"Architects cannot teac[h]

"ARCHITECTS CANNOT TEACH NATURE ANYTHING."
MARK TWAIN

-Mark T[wain]

[Ar]chitects cannot teach nature anything."

Architects cannot teach nat[ure]
anything.
-Mark Twain

Mark Twain

[tho]se wh[o dw]ell among the
[...]s and mysteries of the earth
[ne]ver alone or weary of life."
-Rachel Carson

[Arch]itects cann[ot teach]
[nat]ure anythi[ng."]
[-]Mark Twa[in]

Architects cannot te[ach]

[Ar]chitects cannot teach
nature anything."
-Mark Twain

[Archit]ects cannot teach nature [anything]

-Mark Twain

Architects cannot teach nat[ure]
anything.
Mark Twain

[...]TECTS CANN[OT]

TEACH NATURE

ANYTHING."

... who dwell among the
[...]s and mysteries of the ear[th]

Although this next chapter combines reptiles and amphibians, they are not the same. The most obvious distinguishing trait between these two groups is the fact that only reptiles are covered in scales. Before drawing these animals, it's quite helpful to understand the biological difference between the two.

As diverse as humans are, so are the round, ovular, or diamond-shaped scales that cover the bodies of reptiles. While some scales overlap, others, like mosaic tiles of buildings found in Spain, are placed next to each other as if grout binds them together. The ectothermic blood temperature of reptiles gives them the flexibility of switching between hot and cold. Reptiles are born from eggs; this process can be oviparous (eggs laid and hatched outside of the parent) or ovoviviparous (eggs hatching inside the parental body without placental attachment, making it seem like a live birth).

Although amphibians are also born from eggs, their astounding metamorphosis during their life cycle as well as their smooth, sometimes bumpy skin sets them apart from reptiles. Because amphibians need to keep their skin moist in order to survive, they are quite sensitive to water issues. This makes them an indicator species, which means that you can judge the health of a stream or pond by testing for amphibians. Scientists are witnessing the loss of diversity of amphibians all over the world due to the polluting and damming of streams and rivers. By understanding their role in our ecosystem, we can better understand ours.

When drawing reptiles, note that the way their scales overlap each other suggests the direction in which the reptile is moving. When drawing amphibians, notice the slight gleam of white where light reflects the surface of their body. Draw and shade in the pattern and then erase a streak to get that slimy look.

California Desert Tortoise

(*Gopherus agassizi*)

Desert Tortoises love Prickly Pear Cactus!

Desert Tortoises have sharp claws for digging holes, which serve as shade in a hot, unforgiving desert.

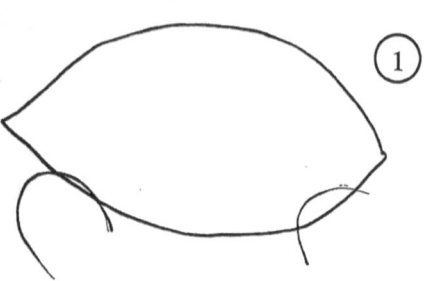

Be careful when driving or doing any recreational activities in the Mojave Desert, as one of the causes of their quick decline is getting crushed by cars and ATVs.

California Desert Tortoises are listed as "threatened" under the Endangered Species Act.

Prickly Pear Cactus
(*Opuntia*)

1

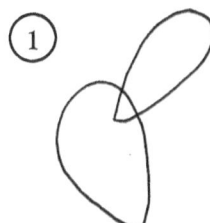

You can use this plant to heal wounds. Just cut off a piece of the cactus pad and apply the flesh to the affected area.

3

2

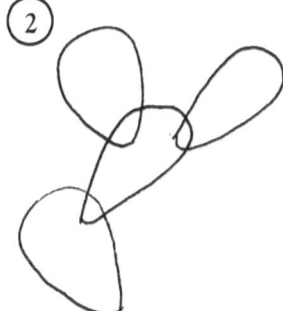

Prickly Pear Cactus fruit provides food for many desert animals, inluding the endangered Desert Tortoise.

4

Be careful not to acquire a new spike wound in the process!

5

Tiger Salamander

(Ambystoma californiense)

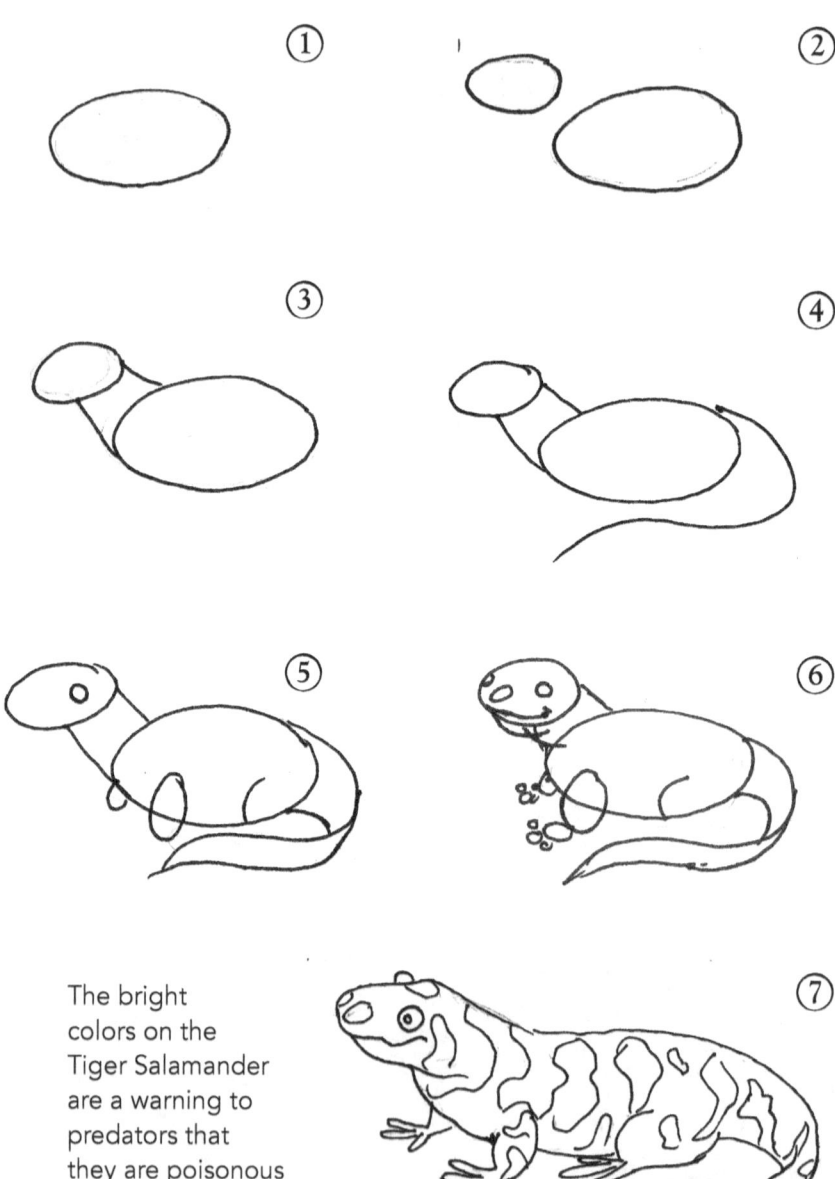

The bright colors on the Tiger Salamander are a warning to predators that they are poisonous to eat.

© Sama Wareh www.warehart.com

Western Toad

(Anaxyrus boreas)

①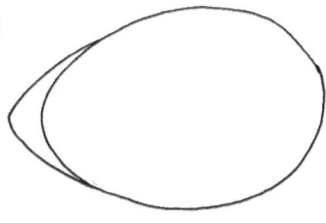

②

③

Western Toads can secrete a mild poison from their glands in order to make their skin taste bitter to predators.

④

Western Fence Lizard

(*Sceloporus occidentalis*)

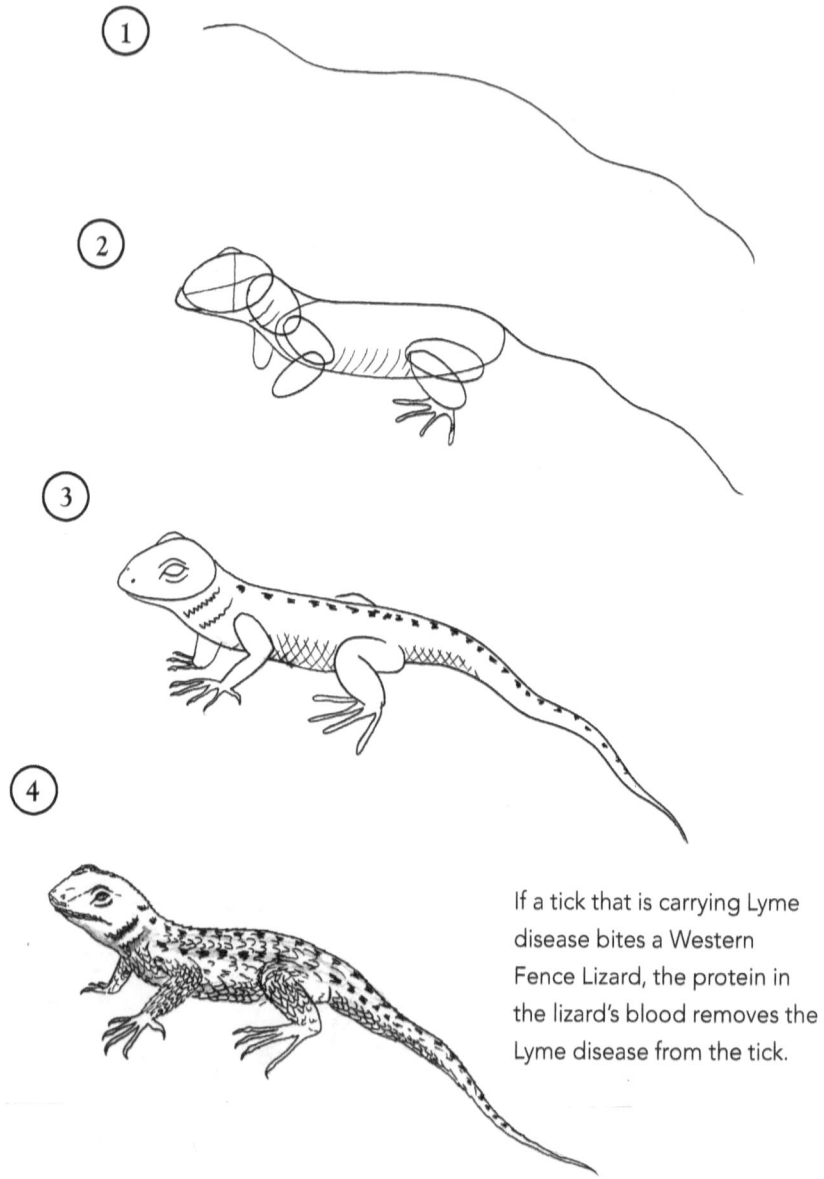

If a tick that is carrying Lyme disease bites a Western Fence Lizard, the protein in the lizard's blood removes the Lyme disease from the tick.

Gopher Snake
(Pituophis catenifer)

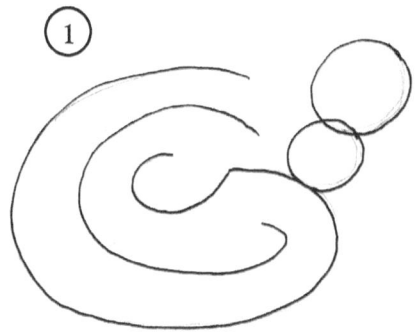

This little copycat likes to pretend to be a rattlesnake by using its tail to "rattle up" the area around it, mimicking a rattlesnake warning.

Coastal Rosy Boa
(*Lichanura trivirgata*)

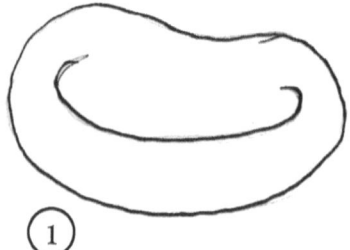

These extremely docile snakes are one of the slowest moving species in the world and for that reason, tend to make excellent pets.

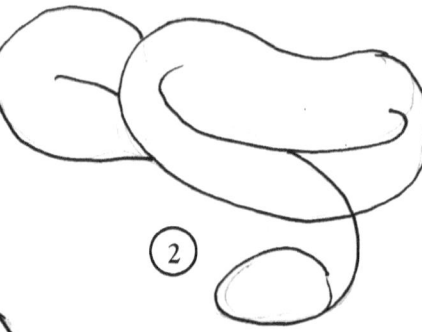

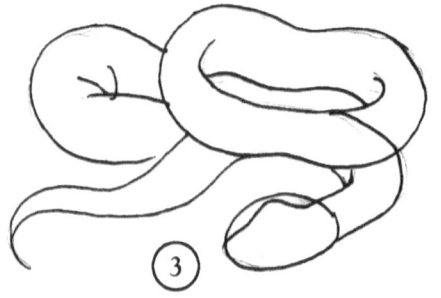

Don't catch one in the wild though, as they are better for the ecosystem than for your house...

California King Snake

(Lampropeltis getula californiae)

These reptiles are called Kings for a reason. They are a predator of poisonous snakes and are immune to their venom.

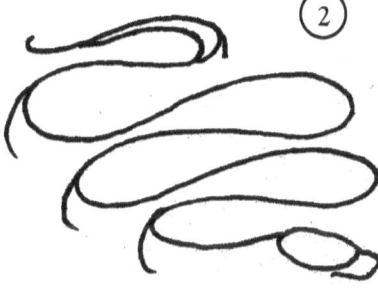

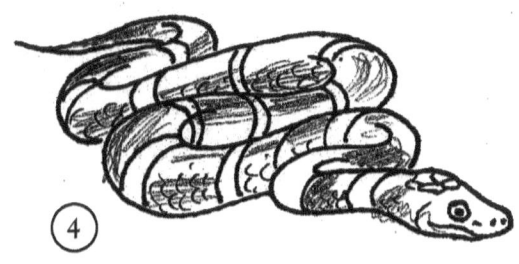

"Those who dwell among the beauties and mysteries of the earth are never alone or weary of life."
-Rachel Carson

Birds

Those who dwell among
the beauties and mysteries
of the earth are never
alone or weary of life.
-Rachel Carson

"THOSE WHO DWELL AMONG THE BEAUTIES AND MYSTERIES
OF THE EARTH ARE NEVER ALONE OR WEARY OF LIFE."
-RACHEL CARSON

e who dwell amor
uties and myste:
e earth are neve
e or weary of life
Rachel Carson

"THOSE WHO DWELL AMONG THE BEAUTIES AND MYSTERIES
OF THE EARTH ARE NEVER ALONE OR WEARY OF LIFE."
-RACHEL CARSON

Those who dwell
among the beauties
and mysteries of the
earth are never
alone or
weary of life."
Rachel Carson

ose who dwell among the
es and mysteries of the earth
ever alone or weary of life."
-Rachel Carson

who dwell amon
d mysterie the earth
alone ury of life."
Rachel Carson

"Those who dwell amon

Birds

Those who dwell among the beauties and mysteries of the earth are never alone or weary of life.
-Rachel Carson

"THOSE WHO DWELL AMONG THE BEAUTIES AND MYSTERIES OF THE EARTH ARE NEVER ALONE OR WEARY OF LIFE."
-RACHEL CARSON

e who dwell amor
auties and myste
e earth are neve
e or weary of life
Rachel Carson

"THOSE WHO DWELL AMONG THE BEAUTIES AND MYSTERIES OF THE EARTH ARE NEVER ALONE OR WEARY OF LIFE."
-RACHEL CARSON

Those who dwell
among the beauties
and mysteries of
earth are never
alone or
weary of life."
Rachel Carson

ose who dwell among the
es and mysteries of the earth
ever alone or weary of life."
-Rachel Carson

who dwell amon
d mysterie
alone   ury of life."
Rachel Carson

ll among
mysterie
e never
y of life.
el Carson

ose w   dwel
the beaut
steries of
are never
alone or
weary of life.'

"Those who dwell among

It's pretty simple when it comes to the characteristics of birds; look for feathers! But to say that birds are simple is a complete travesty. Birds, ranging from insectivores to carnivores, are some of the most fascinating and diverse species on the planet. From the 9-foot wingspan of a California Condor to the 200 miles-per-hour flight of a Peregrine Falcon, the way that each feather is engineered to reflect these animals' traits is a wonder! Unfortunately, as birds are facing more and more threats along the Pacific Flyway, including habitat loss and light pollution, the diversity of our bird species is dwindling. Historically, California was lined with estuaries all along the coast. As the population of California started rising, these wetlands became farmland, housing developments, and roads. Birds play a large part in the dispersal of seeds and contribute to the cheerful soundtrack of the morning sun. Without these magical chirpers and singers, the ecosystem would be as fragile as the wings of a butterfly.

When drawing these birds, envision yourself as an ornithologist who only has but a few seconds to memorize striking features so that they can identify it in their birding guides. Vocalize and describe the features you see on the bird.

Example: A hummingbird has virtually no legs, a jewel covered throat, a long-thin-slightly-curved beak, a flattened helmet looking head, and a small fanned tail. By describing it, you can draw it better and can store it in your memory bank so that you can draw it some other time.

Acorn Woodpecker
(Melanerpes formicivorus)

①

Because of the dense yet spongy bone tissue surrounding its brain, the Acorn Woodpecker is able to withstand the constant drilling of holes without inflicting brain damage.

②

Acorn Woodpeckers love to nest in Sycamore Trees.

③

④

Sycamore Tree
(Acer pseudoplatanus)

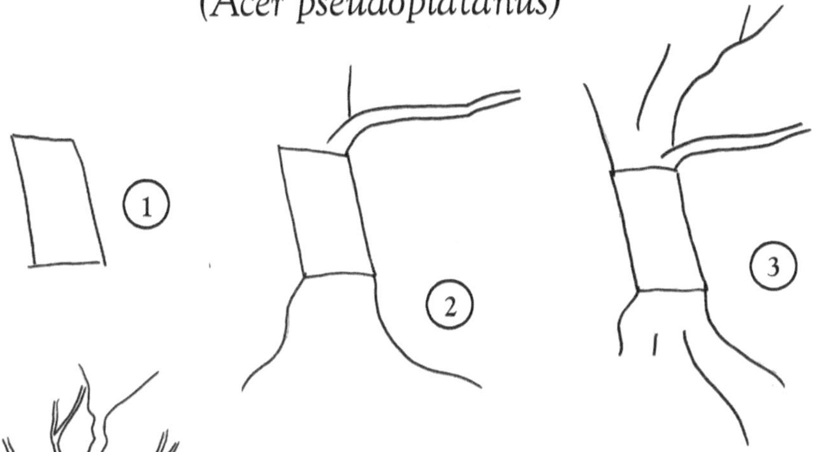

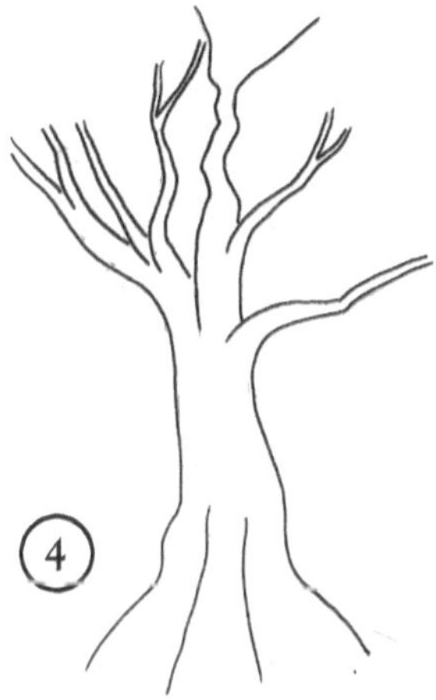

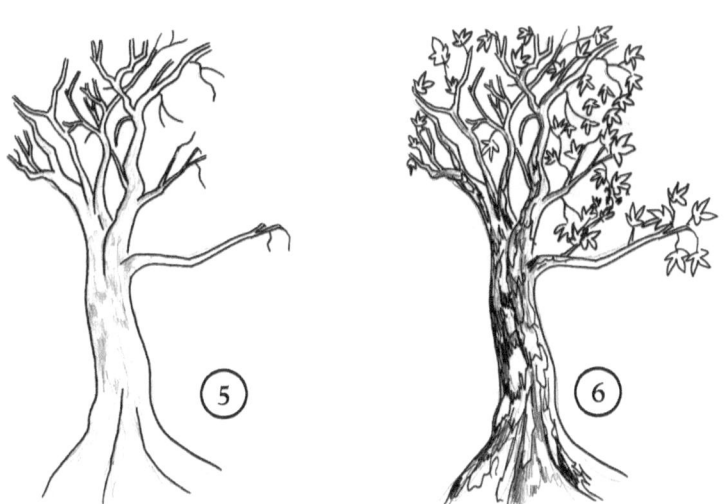

Another name for these trees is "Aliso," which translates to Old Sycamore. They are found in the Riparian ecosystems of Southern California and many of these areas carry the name Aliso in them, such as Aliso Viejo.

Sycamore Trees make an excellent pantry and nesting site for Acorn Woodpeckers.

California Gnatcatcher

(Polioptila californica)

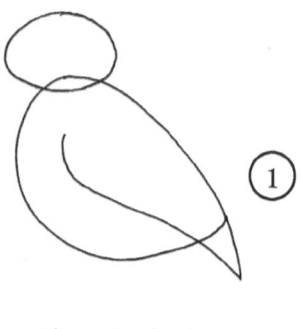

These tiny birds are endangered due to habitat loss, primarily the conversion of Coastal Sage Scrub habitats into land development.

Gnatcatchers need plants like Sagebrush to create their nests.

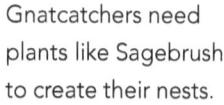

California Sagebrush

(Artemisia californica)

Indigenous families used Sagebrush as an insect repellent by breaking off a piece of the plant and rubbing it all over their bodies.

Sagebrush is a preferred nesting plant for the Gnatcatcher.

①

②

③

④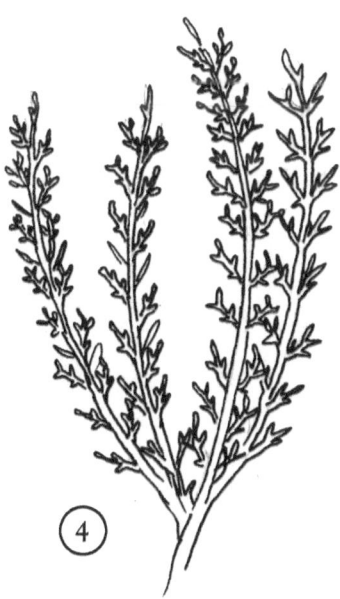

Anna's Hummingbird
(*Calypte anna*)

Hummingbirds are the only group of birds that can fly backwards!

Western Bluebird
(*Sialia mexicana*)

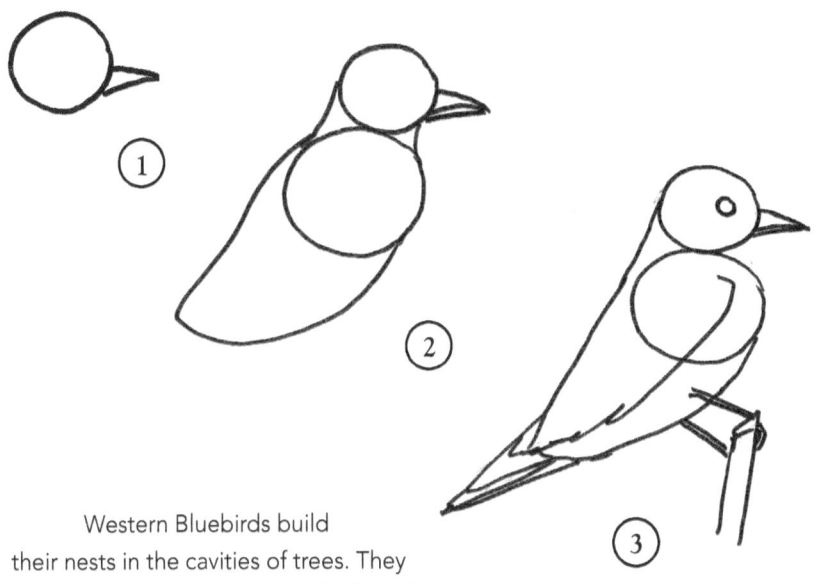

Western Bluebirds build their nests in the cavities of trees. They often rely on dead trees, trunks hollowed out by woodpeckers or man-made nest boxes.

They switch from a main diet of insects in the summertime to fruits and seeds in the wintertime.

California Quail

(Callipepla californica)

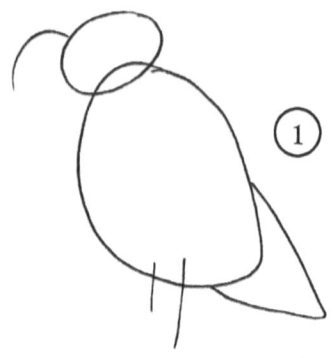

This state bird lives in a social flock known as a covey and participates in a daily communal dust bath.

Greater Roadrunner
(*Geococcyx californianus*)

Roadrunners get their name because of their preference for running over flying. They can run up to 15 miles an hour. They are great for pest control, as they forage for anything from snakes to mice.

Great White Egret
(Ardea alba)

The best way to tell egrets
from storks and cranes
while in flight is that the egrets do
not extend their necks out. They
retract them.

29

Northern Spotted Owl

(*Strix occidentalis*)

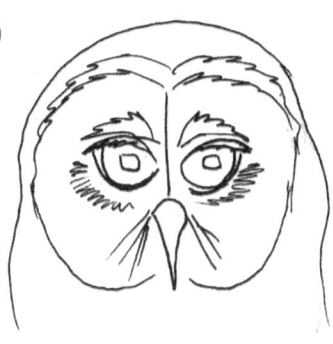

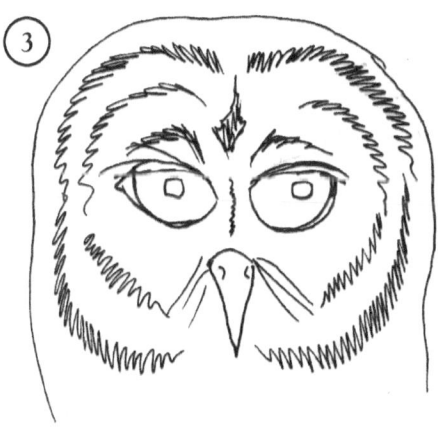

Native to the states of Oregon, Washington, and California, this soft-feathered night watcher was listed as endangered until the regulations on logging became stricter.

Currently, the Northern Spotted Owl is listed as near threatened.

Burrowing Owl
(Athene cunicularia)

Burrowing Owls have a unique insect hunting strategy. They collect scat and deposit it at the entrance to their den as a welcome mat in hopes of attracting insects straight to them.

Great Horned Owl
(Bubo virginianus)

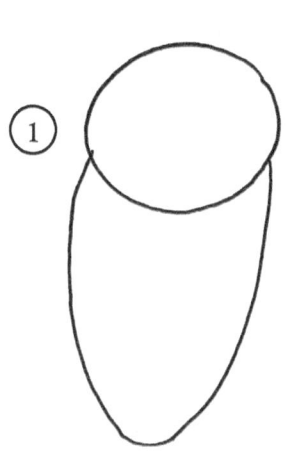

1

2

Don't fall for the "pretend ears" above this Owl's head. They are just tufts of feathers. Great Horned Owls are the largest owls in North America.

3

4

Bald Eagle
(*Haliaeetus leucocephalus*)

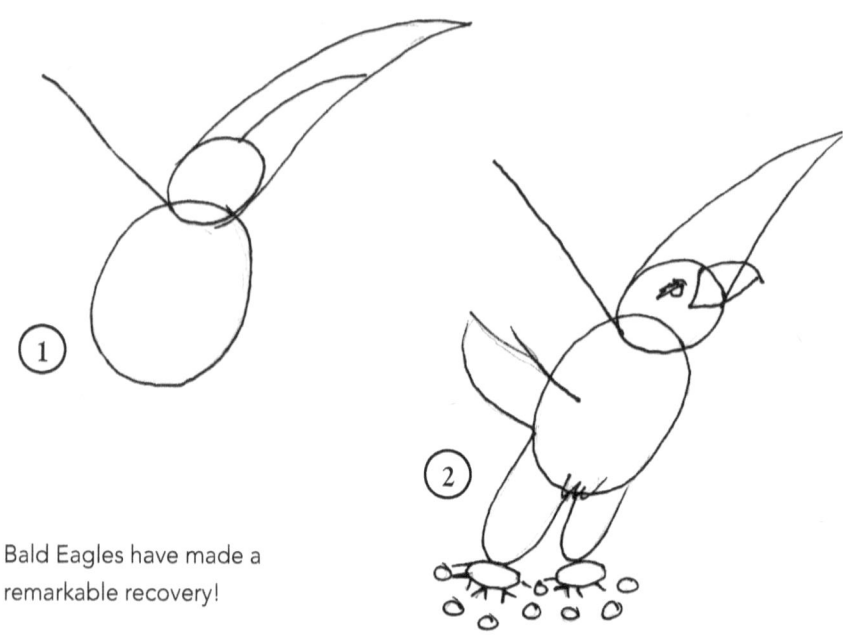

Bald Eagles have made a
remarkable recovery!

They were on the
endangered species list
due to DDT, an insecticide that was
softening their eggshells, causing them to
crack before they were able to hatch. Bald
eagles are no longer endangered due to
several factors, including the
banning of DDT.

Red-Tailed Hawk
(Buteo jamaicensis)

These hawks rely on thermal
updrafts to soar.

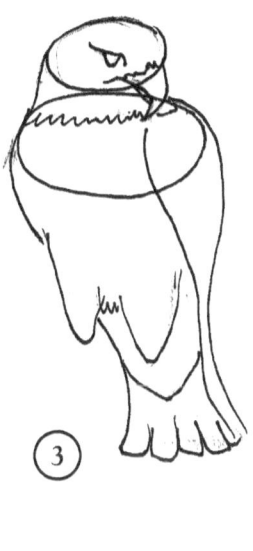

They will keep the same mate for
life and will usually return to the
same nesting spot year after year.

*"When one tugs at a single thing in nature,
he finds it attached to the rest of the world."*
- John Muir

Mammals

"When one tugs at a single thing in nature he finds it attached to the rest of the world."
John Muir

Mammals. We know so much about them, yet so little. What we do know is that they are characterized by many things. Do they have a vertebrate? Do they have hair or fur? Are they endothermic or warm blooded? Do they drink milk after live birth? Do they breathe air with their lungs? These are just a few of the questions we can ask ourselves to identify them. Within each discipline, each trait is its own wonder. Mammals all have their own unique characteristics and adaptations, depending on where they live and what they eat. From the sharp teeth of a puma to the long claws of a sloth, to the fact that most hair on aquatic mammals is around their blowhole, which they are prone to losing as they get older- all fascinating concepts and adaptations.

When drawing mammals, continue with the basic shapes as usual, but at the end of your drawings, be sure to add the hair or fur texture by drawing short line strokes with your pencil. Don't forget that the direction of the lines for the fur helps define the muscular structure of the animal. For animals with short hair, be sure to use tiny line strokes and for animals with long hair, use longer pencil strokes.

Bottlenose Dolphin
(*Tursiops truncatus*)

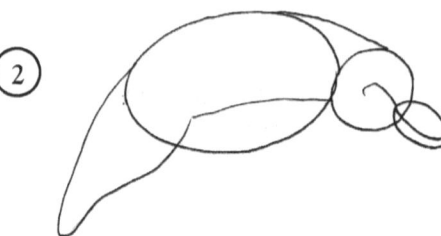

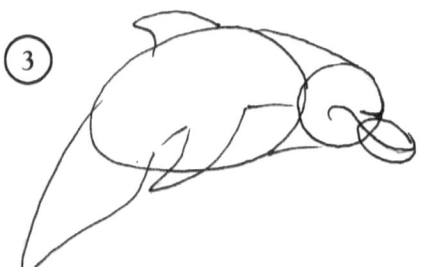

Although dolphins can hold their breath for up to seven minutes, they come up every few minutes for air unless they are sleeping.

Crystal Cove State Park, located in Southern California, is one of the top Bottlenose Dolphin breeding grounds in California.

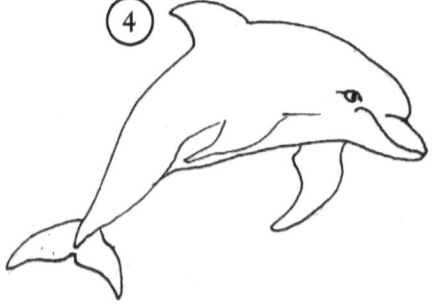

Humpback Whale
(Megaptera novaeangliae)

Humpbacks are a popular type of whale for study, due to the fact that their tails can have different patterns which makes for easy identification of individuals.

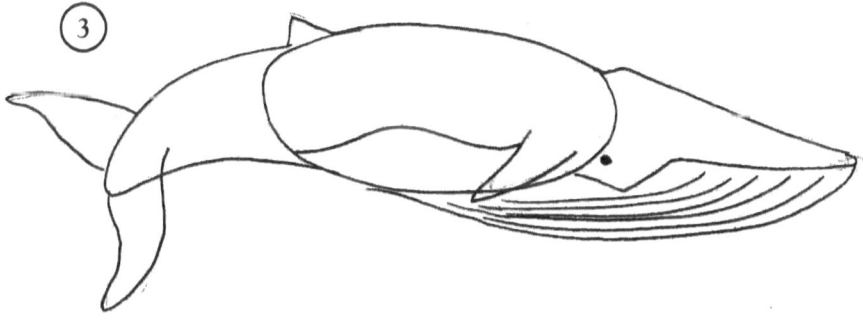

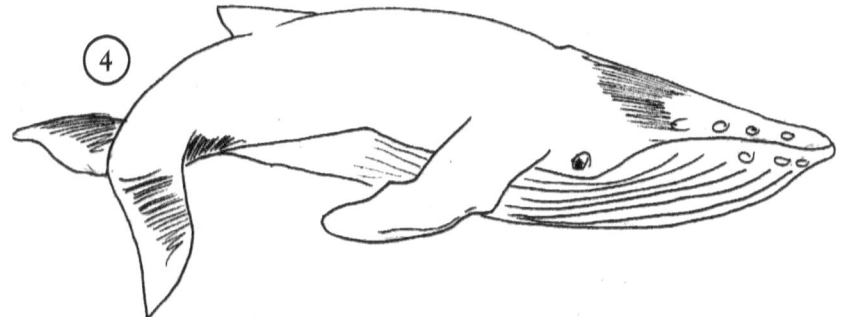

California Grizzly Bear
(*Ursus arctos californicus*)

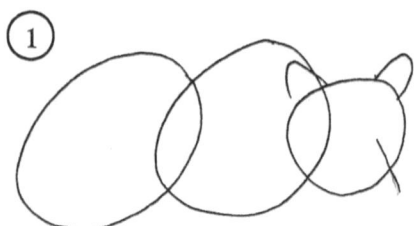

The California Grizzly Bear, although on the California State Flag, has been extinct in California since the early 1900s.

Cottontail Rabbit
(Sylvilagus audubonii)

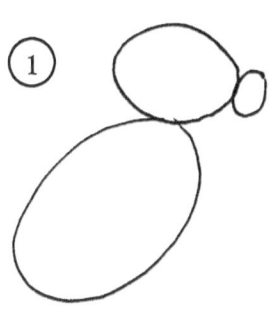

Cottontail Rabbits are named after their fluffy cotton-resembling tails.

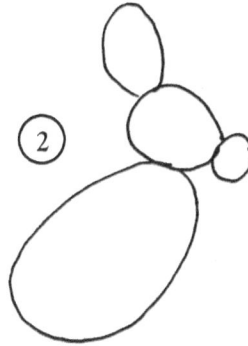

They use their tails as an alarm signal by raising them up to expose the white tuft of fur underneath.

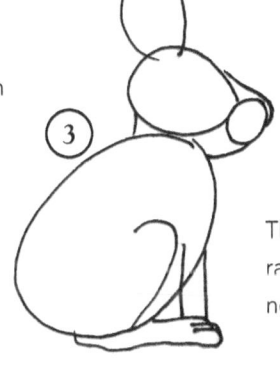

This helps to warn other rabbits that a predator is nearby.

San Joaquin Kit Fox
(*Vulpes macrotis mutica*)

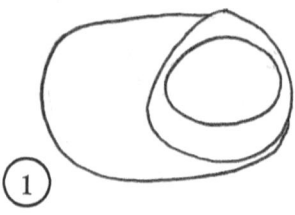

The lifespan of these omnivores is up to 6 years in the wild and 12 in captivity.

It is one of the most endangered animals in California.

Virginia Opossum
(Didelphis virginiana)

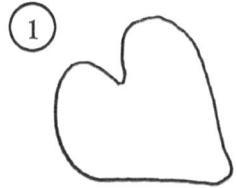

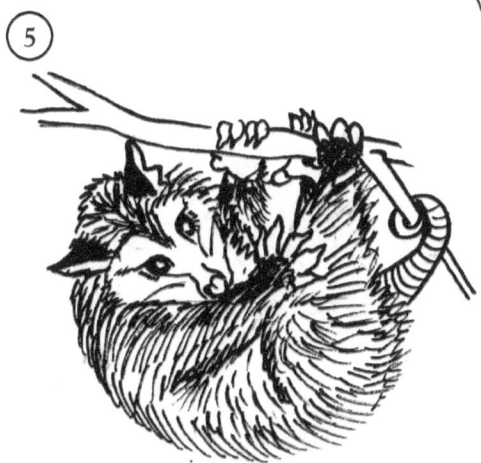

It is quite rare for Opossums to carry rabies, as their body temperature is too low to host the virus.

Bobcat
(Lynx rufus)

Bobcats are named for their short tail.

Dusky-Footed Wood Rat
(*Neotoma fuscipes*)

①

These rats build their nest by laying down branches and sticks and then adhering them together with their own scat.

They disguise the scent of their den with plants, usually some sort of strong-smelling plant such as sage.

②

③

Coyote
(Canis latrans)

①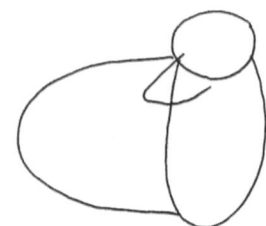

②

③

In traditional aboriginal legends, the Coyote is often represented as the clever trickster.

④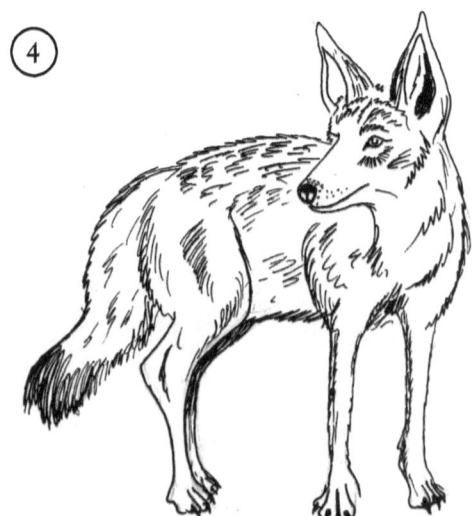

On another note, having Coyote as your totem animal is often symbolic of being easily adaptable to change, just as Coyotes are.

California Ground Squirrel
(*Otospermophilus beecheyi*)

Ground Squirrels will try to disguise their scent to rattlesnakes by chewing on the old shedding of the snake, then licking themselves and their babies.

Mountain Lion
(Puma concolor)

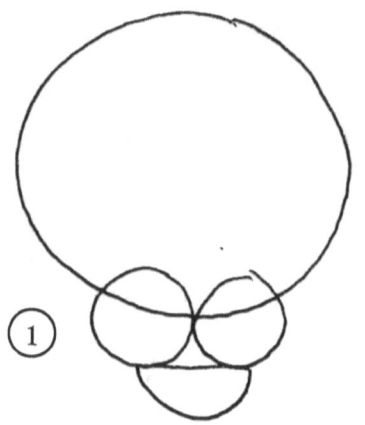

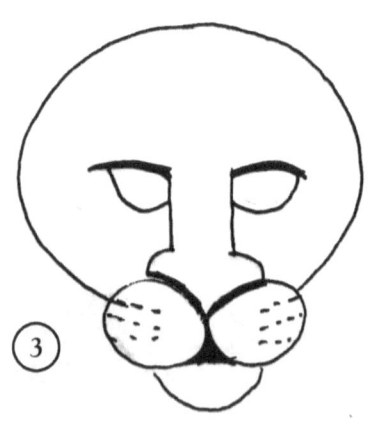

If you ever see a Mountain Lion in the wild, the best thing to do is freeze, raise both hands in the air, yell as loudly as you can, and sound as threatening as possible. If you run, you could end up being fast food.

Mule Deer
(*Odocoileus hemionus*)

This herbivore gets its name from its large, mule-like ears.

①

②

③

A fun way to remember if an animal is predator or prey is by memorizing this rhyme:

Eyes in front, likes to hunt.
Eyes on the side, likes to hide.

"Nature will bear the closest inspection. She invites us to lay our eye level with her smallest leaf, and take an insect view of its plain."
- Henry David Thoreau

Arthropods

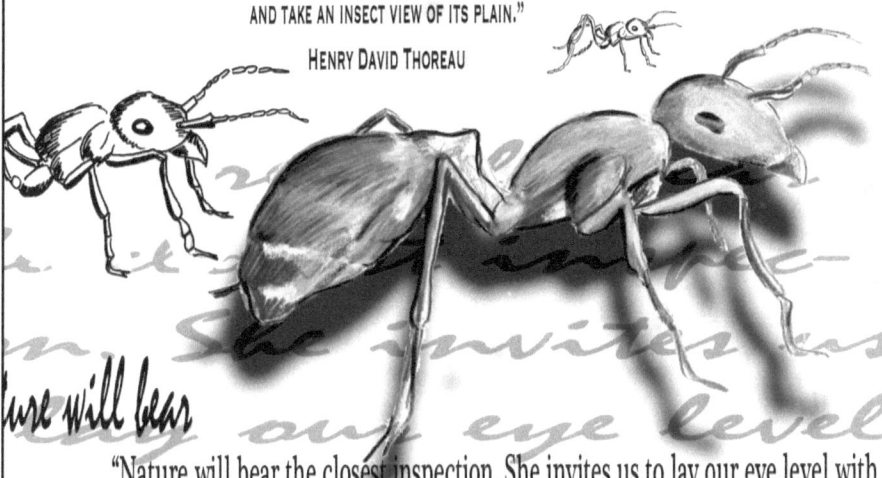

"NATURE WILL BEAR THE CLOSEST INSPECTION. SHE INVITES US TO LAY OUR EYE LEVEL WITH HER SMALLEST LEAF, AND TAKE AN INSECT VIEW OF ITS PLAIN."

HENRY DAVID THOREAU

"Nature will bear the closest inspection. She invites us to lay our eye level with her smallest leaf, and take an insect view of its plain."

Henry David Thoreau

Nature will bear the closest inspec- tion. She invites us to lay our eye level

NATURE WILL BEAR THE CLOSEST INSPECTION. SHE INVITES US T
AND TAKE AN INSECT VIEW OF
HENRY DAVID THOR

Nature will bear the closest inspec- tion. She invites us to lay our eye level

Arthropods

"NATURE WILL BEAR THE CLOSEST INSPECTION. SHE INVITES US TO LAY OUR EYE LEVEL WITH HER SMALLEST LEAF,
AND TAKE AN INSECT VIEW OF ITS PLAIN."
HENRY DAVID THOREAU

"Nature will bear the closest inspection. She invites us to lay our eye level with her smallest leaf, and take an insect view of its plain."

Henry David Thoreau

Nature will bear

the closest inspec-

tion. She invites us

to lay our eye level

Arthro means jointed and pod means leg, so Arthropods are creatures with many jointed legs. This includes crustaceans, spiders, and insects. Arthropods, with over a million different species ranging from the tiniest microscopic plankton to large ocean dwelling lobsters, have an exoskeleton which they need to molt in order to grow larger. Arthropods are the heartbeat of our ecosystem, the grinding wheel that keeps everything turning. Without Arthropods, dead things would litter the planet, pollination would not be a reality, and the indirect fuel to sustain the top consumers would be lost. I like to think of the Arachnids as the police officers of the insect kingdom, monitoring the population of these six-legged creatures, and keeping things under control. Each Arthropod has unique colors and designs on its segmented body. The next time a bee lands on you, instead of flicking it off, take the opportunity to observe it up close and you'll be amazed at the details of design found in the bee, from its compound eyes to the hair on its body.

When drawing Arthropods, start with the basic shapes of the segmented body parts and then begin infusing symmetry into it. While some Arthropods have bristles or hair on their thorax, others have a glossy outer cover.

California Harvester Ant
(Pogonomyrmex californicus)

The primary meal for The Coast Horned
Lizard, these ants seal off their nests
during the wintertime.

Their numbers have been declining due
to invasive species such as the aggressive
Argentine Ants taking over their territory.

Yeah, Argentine Ants are those ants
that invade your home if you leave
one crumb out!

Coast Horned Lizard

(Phrynosoma coronatum)

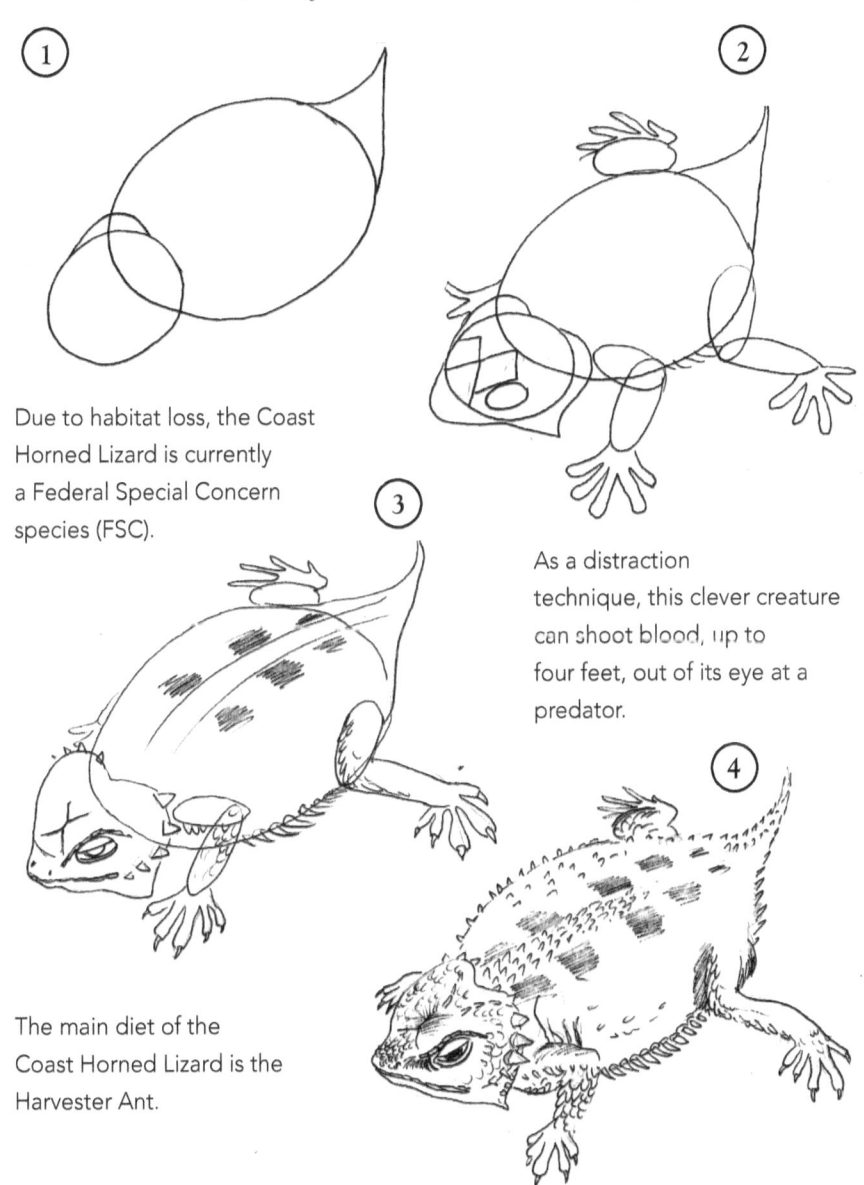

Due to habitat loss, the Coast Horned Lizard is currently a Federal Special Concern species (FSC).

As a distraction technique, this clever creature can shoot blood, up to four feet, out of its eye at a predator.

The main diet of the Coast Horned Lizard is the Harvester Ant.

Monarch Caterpillar

(*Danaus plexippus*)

①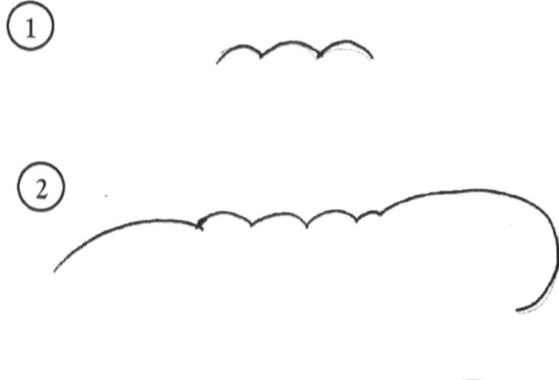

After two weeks of being a caterpillar, this striped insect transforms into a chrysalis for approximately 10 days before emerging as a butterfly.

②

③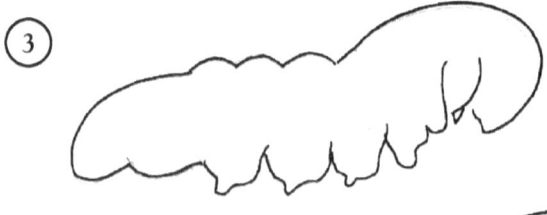

Next time you complain about too much change in your life, remember the caterpillar.

④

⑤

Golden - Orb Weaver
(Argiope aurantia)

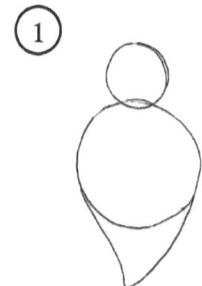

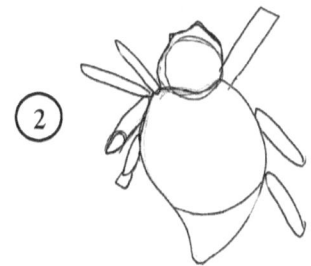

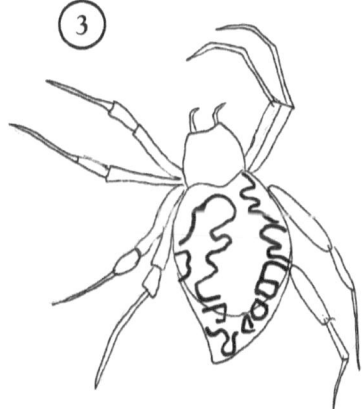

These large spiders tend to appear in fields and gardens, adorning pathways with huge, intricate webs.

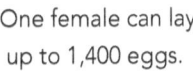

One female can lay up to 1,400 eggs.

"There is nothing in a caterpillar that tells you it's going to be a butterfly."
-Richard Buckminster Fuller

Butterflies & Their Host Plants

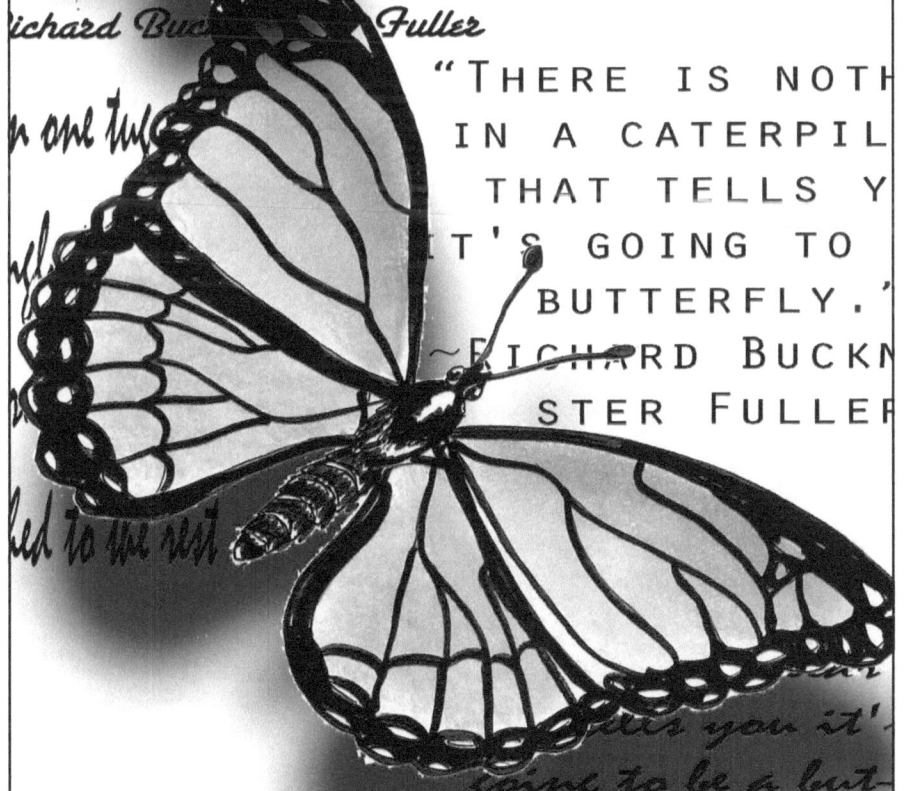

"There is nothing in a caterpillar that tells you it's going to be a butterfly."
-Richard Buckminster Fuller

"There is nothing in a caterpillar that tells you it's going to be a butterfly."
~Richard Buckminster Fuller

"There is nothing in a caterpillar that tells you it's going to be a butterfly."
-Richard Buckminster Fuller

"THERE IS NOTHING IN A CATERPILLAR THAT TELLS YOU IT'S GOING TO BE A BUTTERFLY."
~RICHARD BUCKMINSTER FULLER

Butterflies & Their Host Plants

"There is nothing in a caterpillar that tells you it's going to be a butterfly."
-Richard Buckminster Fuller

"There is nothing in a caterpillar that tells you it's going to be a butterfly."
~Richard Buckminster Fuller

"There is nothing in ... tells you it's going ~Richard Buck...

...ing in a ...erpillar that tells you it's going to be a ...utterfly.

...ichard Buc... ...Fuller

"THERE IS NOTH... IN A CATERPIL... THAT TELLS Y... ...T'S GOING TO ... BUTTERFLY.' ~...ICHARD BUCKM... ...STER FULLER

As children, we were immediately drawn to the beauty of butterflies. Perhaps it's because they remind us of fairies or because we are drawn in by the diversity of their colors and the shapes of their wings. These whimsical flower adornments have interesting life cycles, and perhaps that is what intrigues us most. Their four-stage life cycle, from egg to larvae, to chrysalis, to butterfly is a mystery to us. Scientists still wonder at how the cells restructure to form the butterfly. On a symbolic level, butterflies represent having to sacrifice something in order to attain something greater. These butterflies, a constant reminder to humans that change is very much a part of life, are pollinators and help with the cycle of growth.

The most well known California butterfly is the Monarch butterfly, with its interesting migration patterns between Canada and Mexico. The first three generations of Monarchs have a life cycle between 6 to 8 weeks, while the fourth generation, which completes the migration journey, can live between 6 - 8 months. Some findings have indicated that there may be a fifth generation. We can help ensure the success of their migration by replanting native and butterfly host plants.

When trying to draw butterflies, it's easiest if you work on both sides of the wings at the same time. In other words, if you draw one line on one side, add the other line on the other side so that symmetry can be maintained.

Buckeye Butterfly
(Junonia coenia)

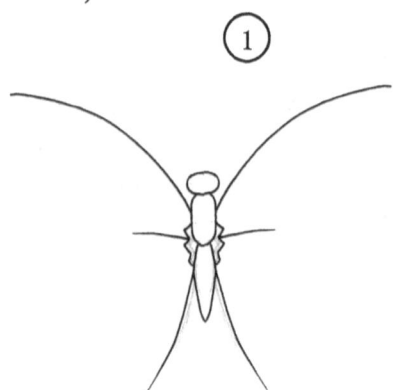

①

This butterfly enjoys open, sunny areas with short, shrubby plants.

②

The host plants for the Buckeye Butterfly include the Monkey flower of the Mimulus species, Plantago lanceolata, and the Antirrhinum species, Snapdragon.

③

The eyespots on this butterfly serve to scare away predators.

Black Sage
(*Salvia mellifera*)

Black Sage is a nectar plant for the Buckeye butterfly.

A cold cup of Black Sage tea is used as a stomach tonic to cure ulcers.

*See page 89

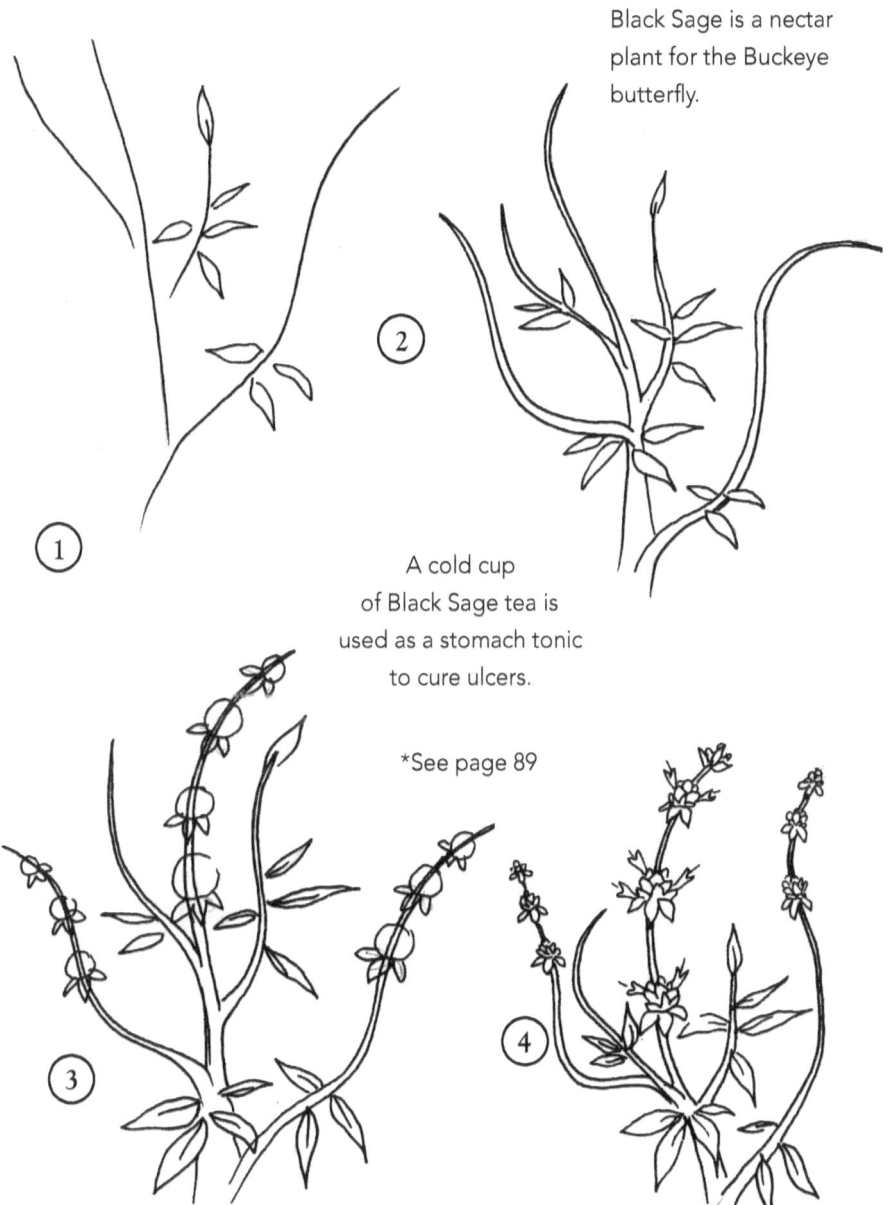

California Dogface
(*Zerene eurydice*)

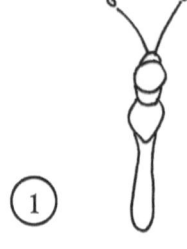

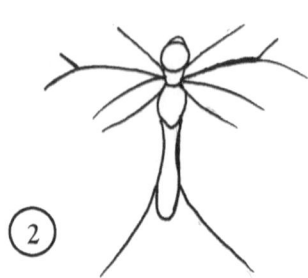

Sexually dimorphic, male Dogface butterflies are a much brighter yellow with black-tipped upper wings.

Nectar plants include Wooly Blue Curls, White & Black Sage, and California Fuchsia.

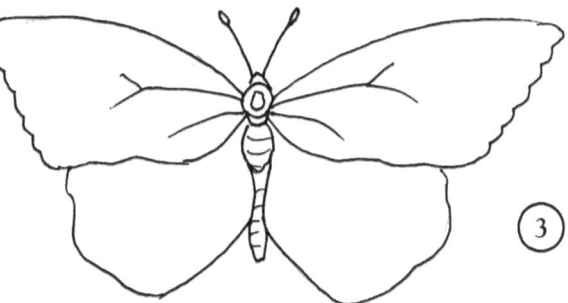

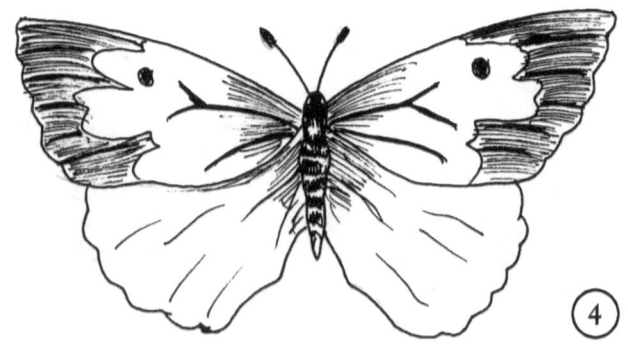

False Indigo
(Amorpha fruticosa)

This shrubby bush is the host plant for the California Dogface butterfly.

Monarch Butterfly
(*Danaus plexippus*)

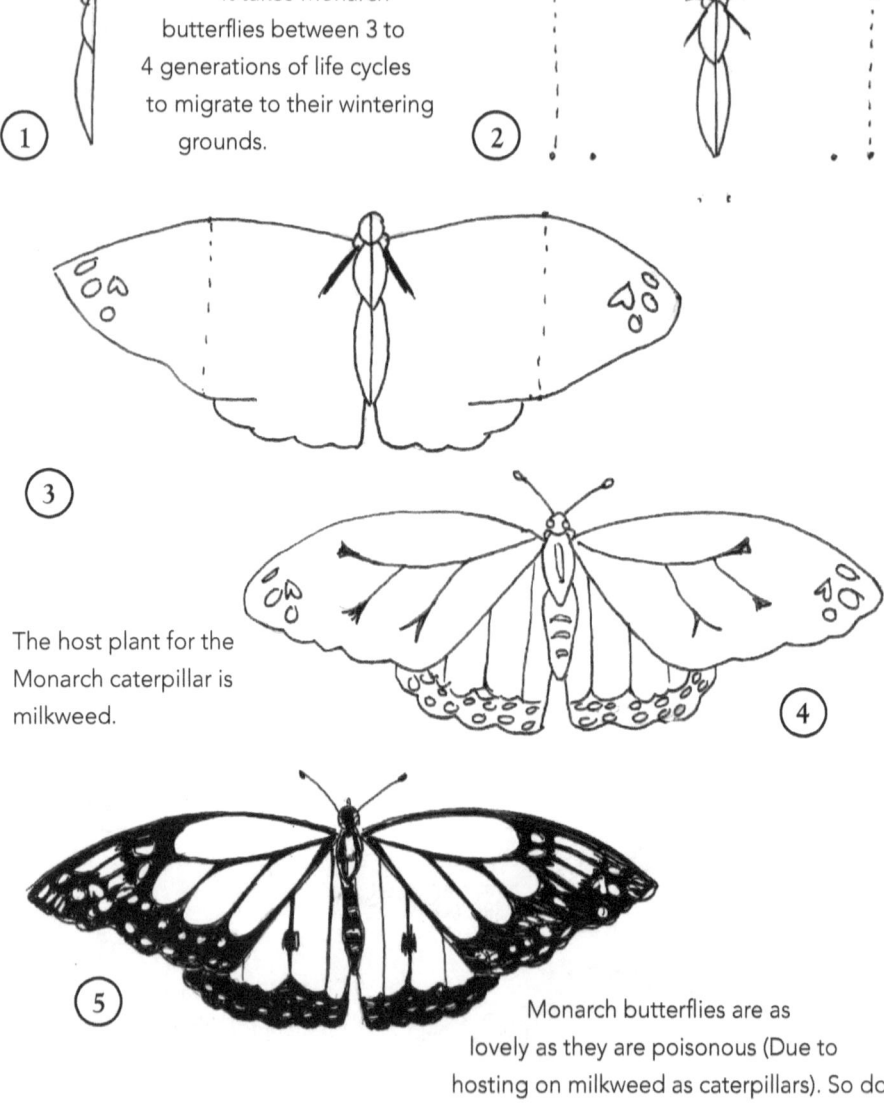

It takes Monarch butterflies between 3 to 4 generations of life cycles to migrate to their wintering grounds.

1

2

3

The host plant for the Monarch caterpillar is milkweed.

4

5

Monarch butterflies are as lovely as they are poisonous (Due to hosting on milkweed as caterpillars). So do yourself a favor and don't eat one.

Narrow Leaf Milkweed
(Asclepias fascicularis)

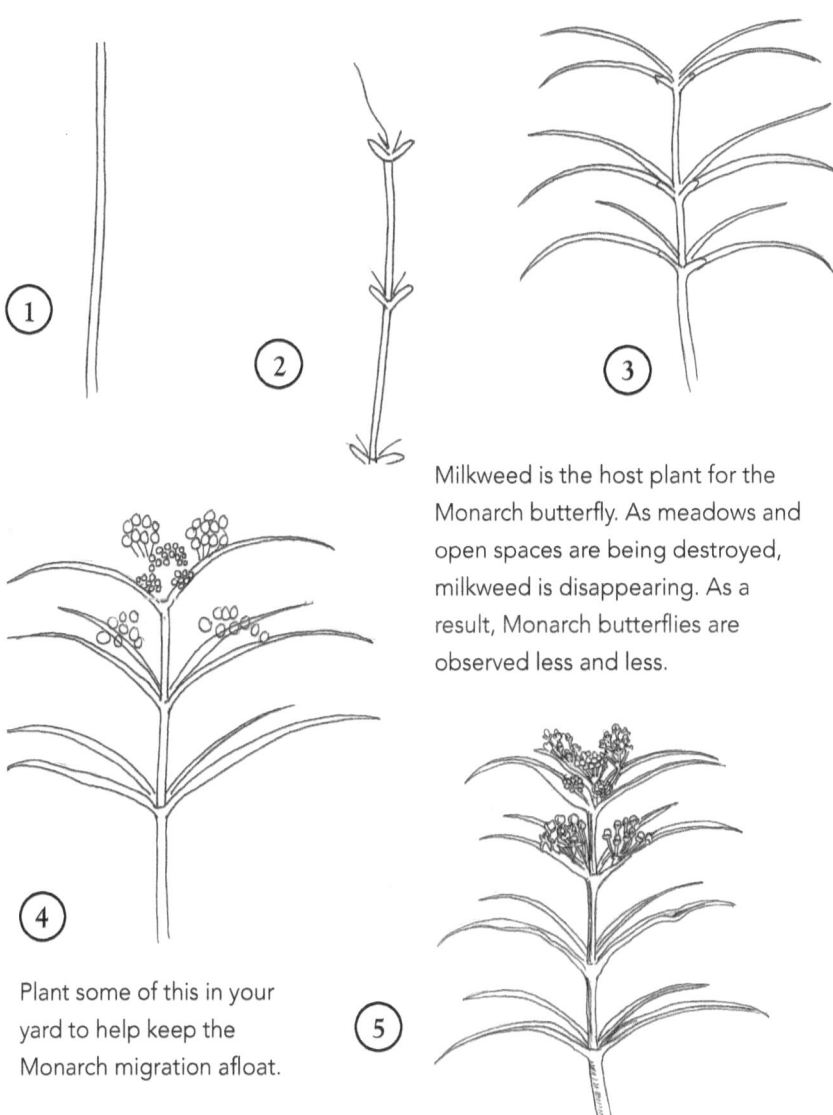

Milkweed is the host plant for the Monarch butterfly. As meadows and open spaces are being destroyed, milkweed is disappearing. As a result, Monarch butterflies are observed less and less.

Plant some of this in your yard to help keep the Monarch migration afloat.

American Painted Lady Butterfly
(*Vanessa virginiensis*)

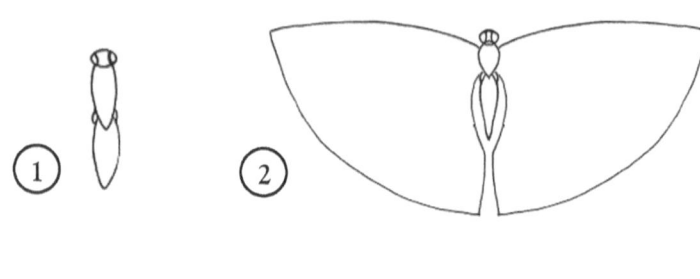

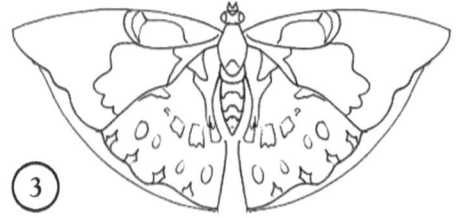

These are popular classroom butterflies because of how easy it is to keep them.

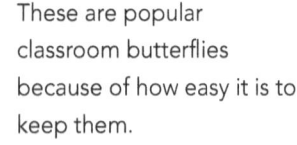

© Sama Wareh www.warehart.com

Pearly Everlasting
(Anaphalis margaritacea)

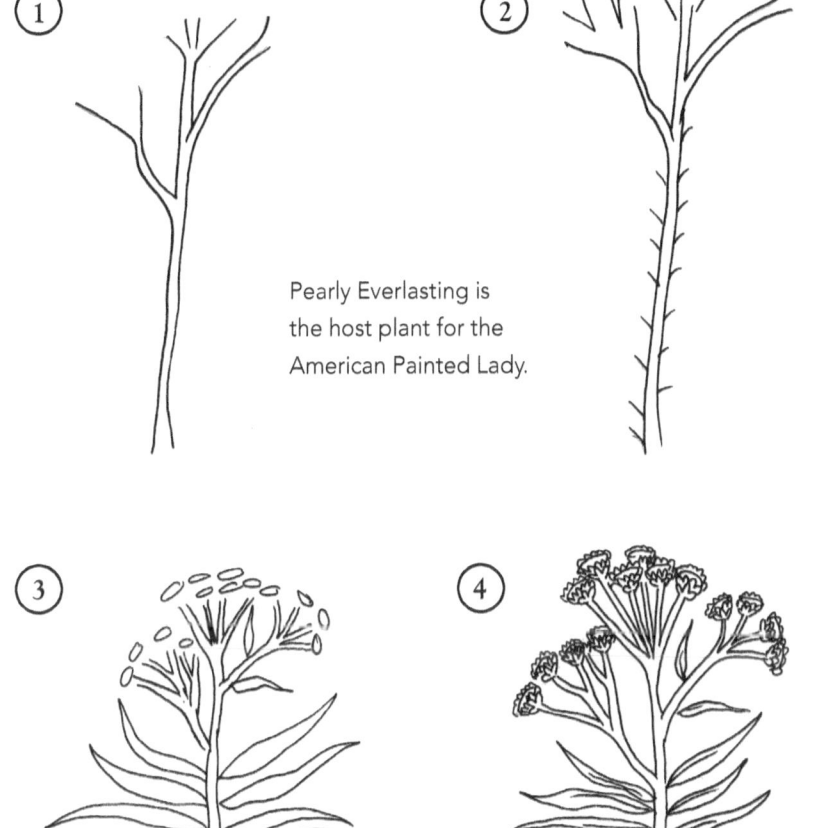

Pearly Everlasting is
the host plant for the
American Painted Lady.

Lorquin's Admiral
(*Limenitis lorquini*)

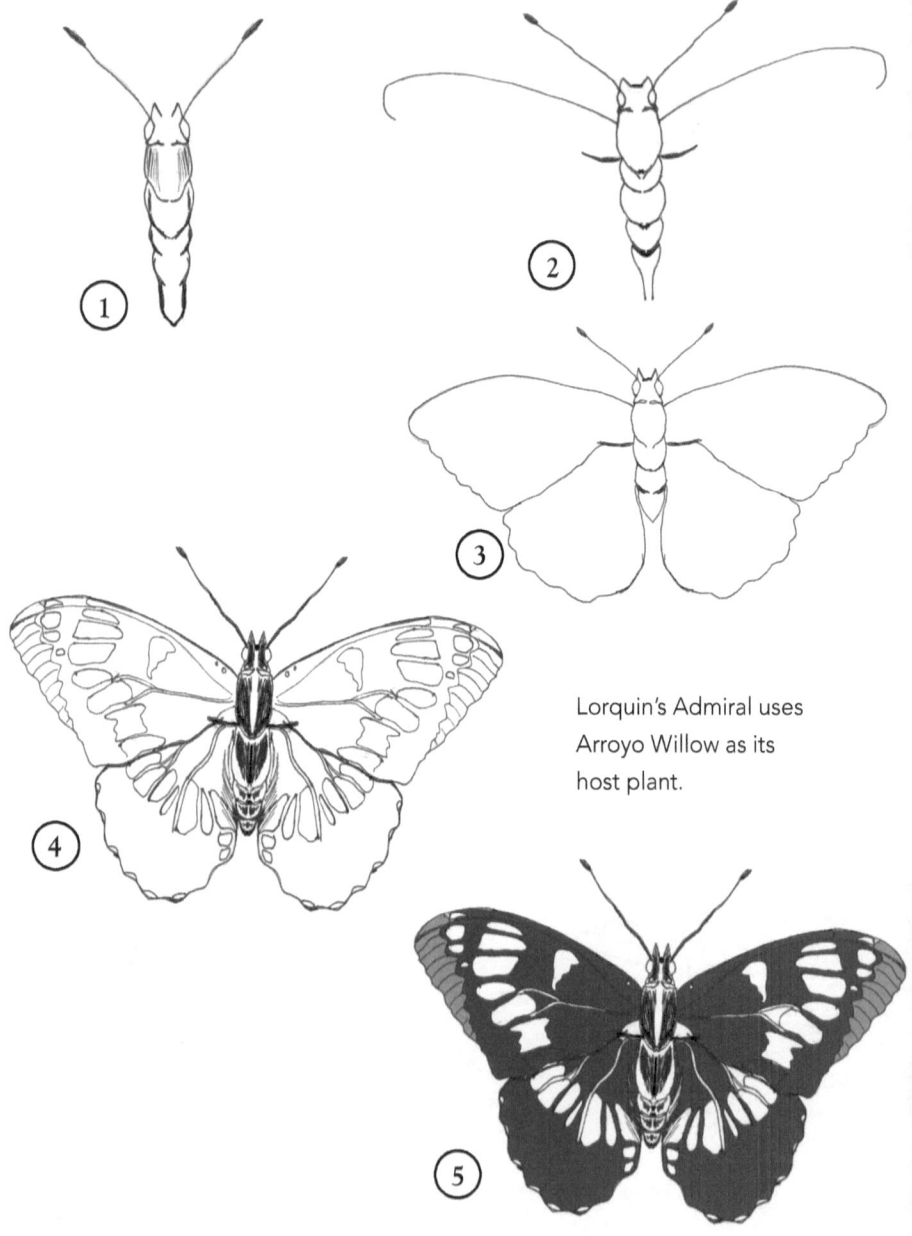

Lorquin's Admiral uses
Arroyo Willow as its
host plant.

Western Tiger Swallowtail
(Papilio rutulus)

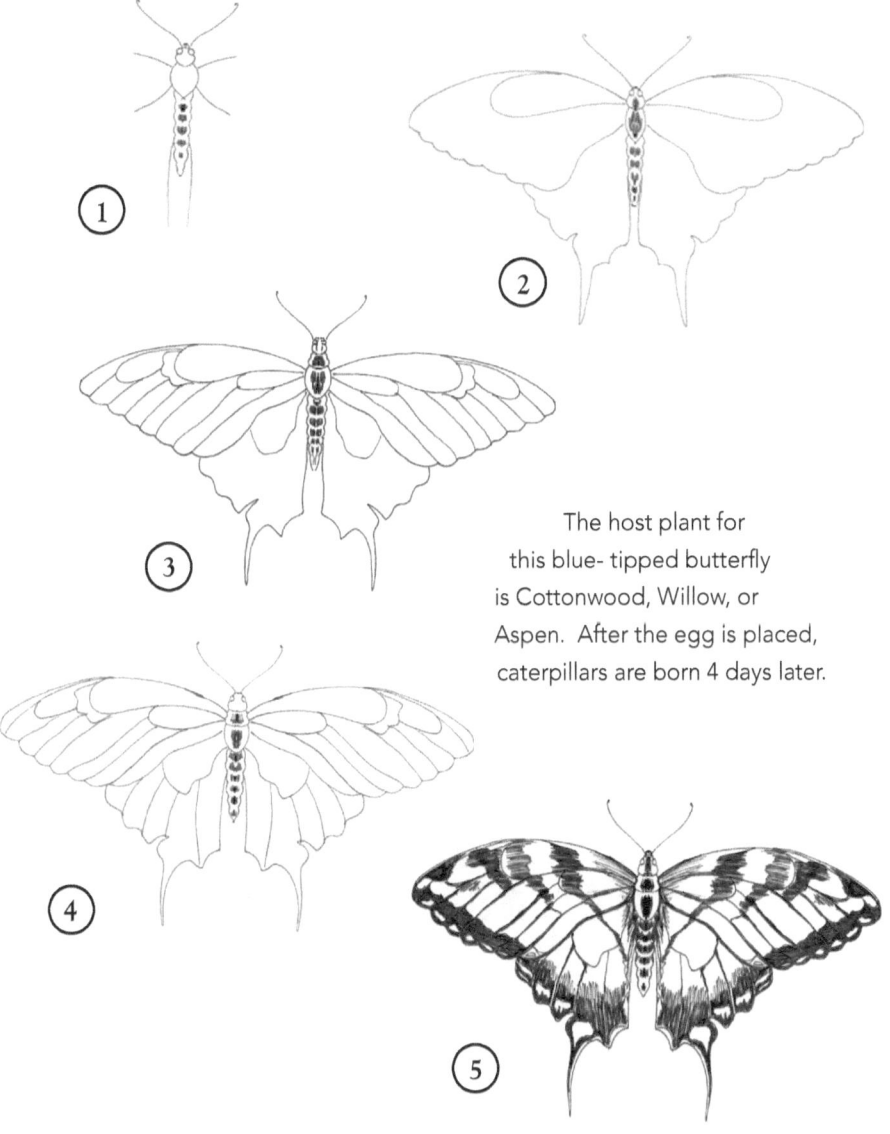

The host plant for this blue- tipped butterfly is Cottonwood, Willow, or Aspen. After the egg is placed, caterpillars are born 4 days later.

Mourning Cloak Butterfly
(*Nymphalis antiopa antiopa*)

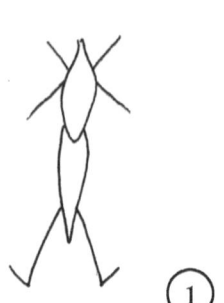

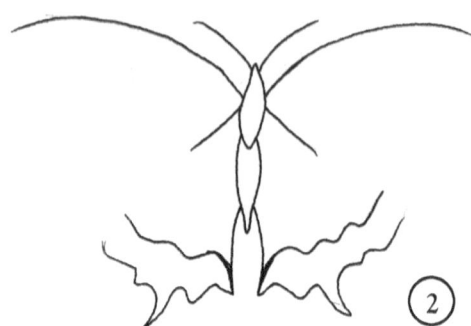

These butterflies have specialized glycerol blood, which acts like antifreeze and helps them raise their body temperature during the wintertime.

Arroyo Willow
(Salix lasiolepis)

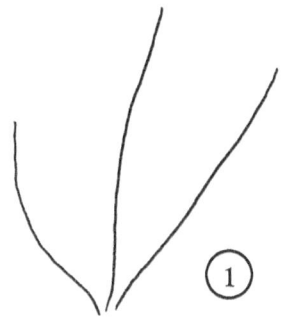

Arroyo Willow is the host plant for the Lorquin's Admiral, Western Tiger Swallowtail, and the Mourning Cloak Butterflies.

The indigenous tribes used to chew on the bark as it provided an excellent headache relief.

"The art of medicine consists of amusing the patient while Nature cures the disease."
Voltaire

Plants

"The art of medicine consists of amusing the patient while Nature cures the disease."

Voltaire

e art of medicine consists of amusing the atient while Nature cures the disease."

Voltaire

e art of ... "The art of med ... edicine ... amusing the patient ... the disease.

edicine consists of amusing the patient le Nature cures the disease."

— Voltaire

"The art of medicine

onsists of amusing the

ient while Nature cures

the disease."

-VOLTAIRE

"THE ART
MEDICINE CON
OF AMUSING
PATIENT WH
NATURE CURE
DISEASE.
-VOLTAIR

""The art o

medicine cons

of amusing t

Plants

"The art of medicine consists
of amusing the patient while
Nature cures the disease."
Voltaire

e art of medicine consists of amusing the
atient while Nature cures the disease."
Voltaire

e art of
edicine

"The art of med
amusing the patient
the disease.

edicine consists of amusing the patient
ile Nature cures the disease."
- Voltaire

" "THE ART
MEDICINE CON
OF AMUSING
PATIENT WH
NATURE CURE
DISEASE.
-VOLTAIR

"The art of medicine

onsists of amusing the

ient while Nature cures

the disease."

VOLTAIRE

" "The art o

medicine cons

of amusing t

California's terrain is extremely diverse. You will find a dramatic change in the ecosystem and plant community in just a two hour drive from almost anywhere. From the Mojave Desert to the Sequoia Avenue of the Giants, California's beauty and captivating lure, is the idea that you can practically ski and surf in the same day.

The chaparral, desert, and coastal sage scrub communities have drought-tolerant plants. Although many of these plants look dry, they actually are not, and have light colors in order to retain water. The downside of the dull colors is that it leads local California residents to believe that these un-colorful plants should be replaced with more "exotic" rainforest plants, which is a direct strain on our water supply in California. Native plants are everything we need; keeping them here ensures the preservation of birds along their migratory path and the conservation of native animals.

Plants are a tricky thing to draw, and what fascinates me most about plants is that the perfection of them lies in their imperfection, a gentle reminder that it's okay to be imperfect as long as there is balance. Each leaf is symmetrical and each plant has a set design, although they each have stems branching out in different directions and off-centered flower heads seeking recognition. When drawing these plants, bear in mind that many leaves have upside down tear drop shapes and point in opposite directions.

Bush Sunflower
(Encelia californica)

Blooms
December
through
June and is
extremely
drought
tolerant.

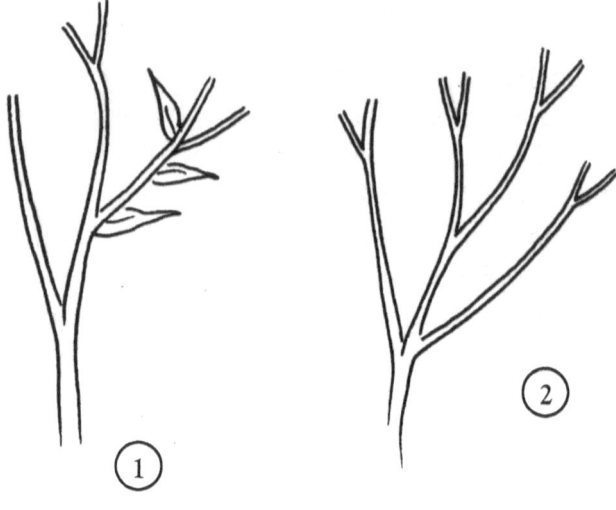

California Buckwheat

(Eriogonum fasciculatum)

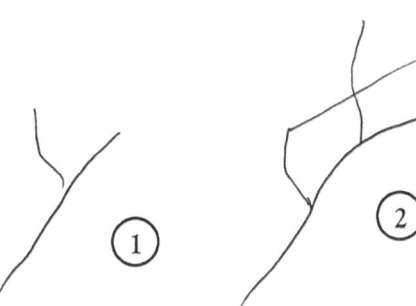

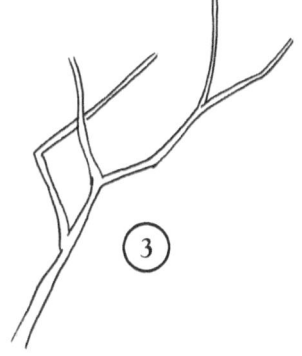

Buckwheat was used by the indigenous families of California in many ways. From food to tea, this drought-tolerant, gluten-free plant is a multi-purpose treasure.

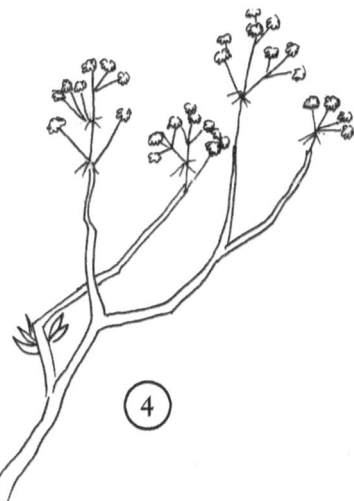

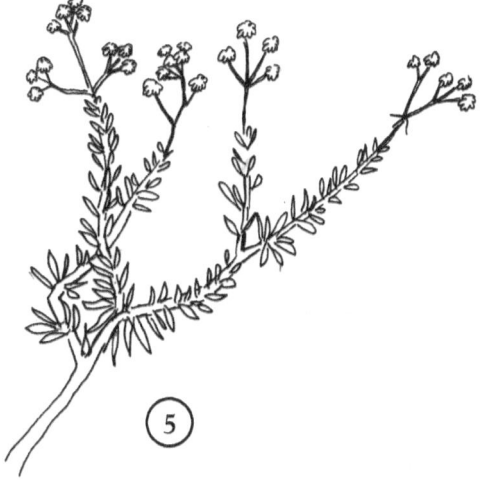

Dried flower seeds of buckwheat can be roasted and made into tea.

*See page 89

California Poppy
(*Eschscholzia californica*)

California Poppy is the official state flower of California.

California Wild Rose

(Rosa californica)

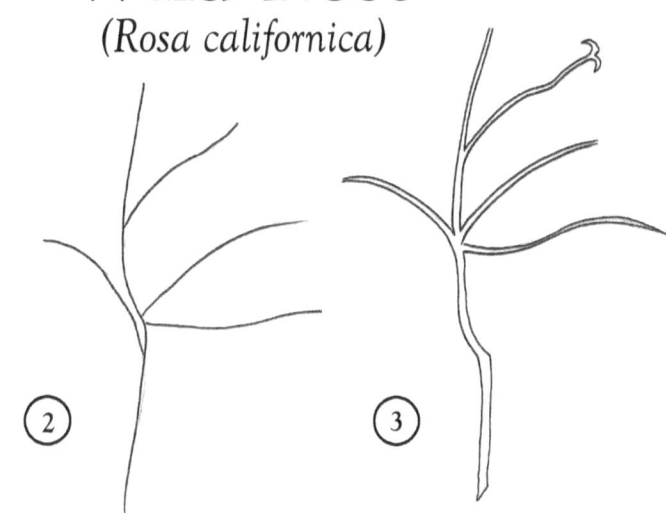

The rose hips of this plant, which look like miniature apples, have more vitamin C than an orange!

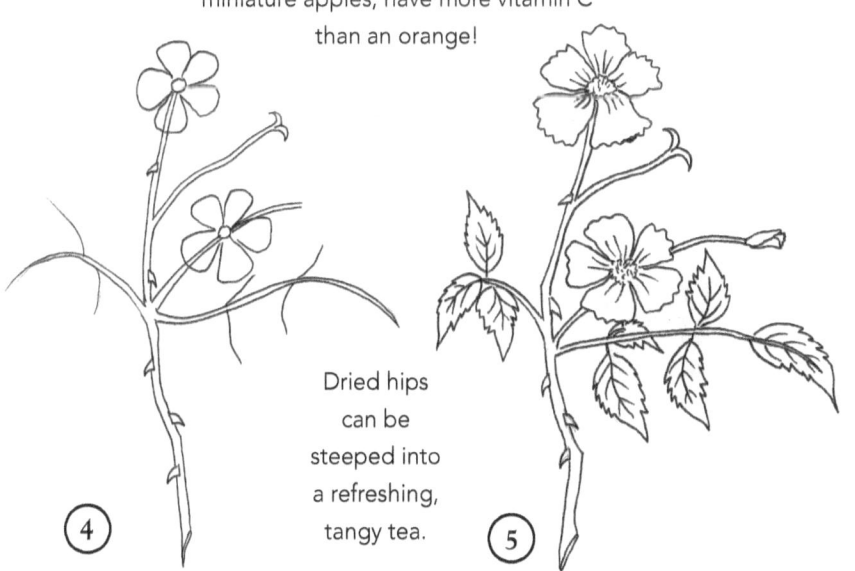

Dried hips can be steeped into a refreshing, tangy tea.

*See page 90

Chaparral Yucca
(*Hesperoyucca whipplei*)

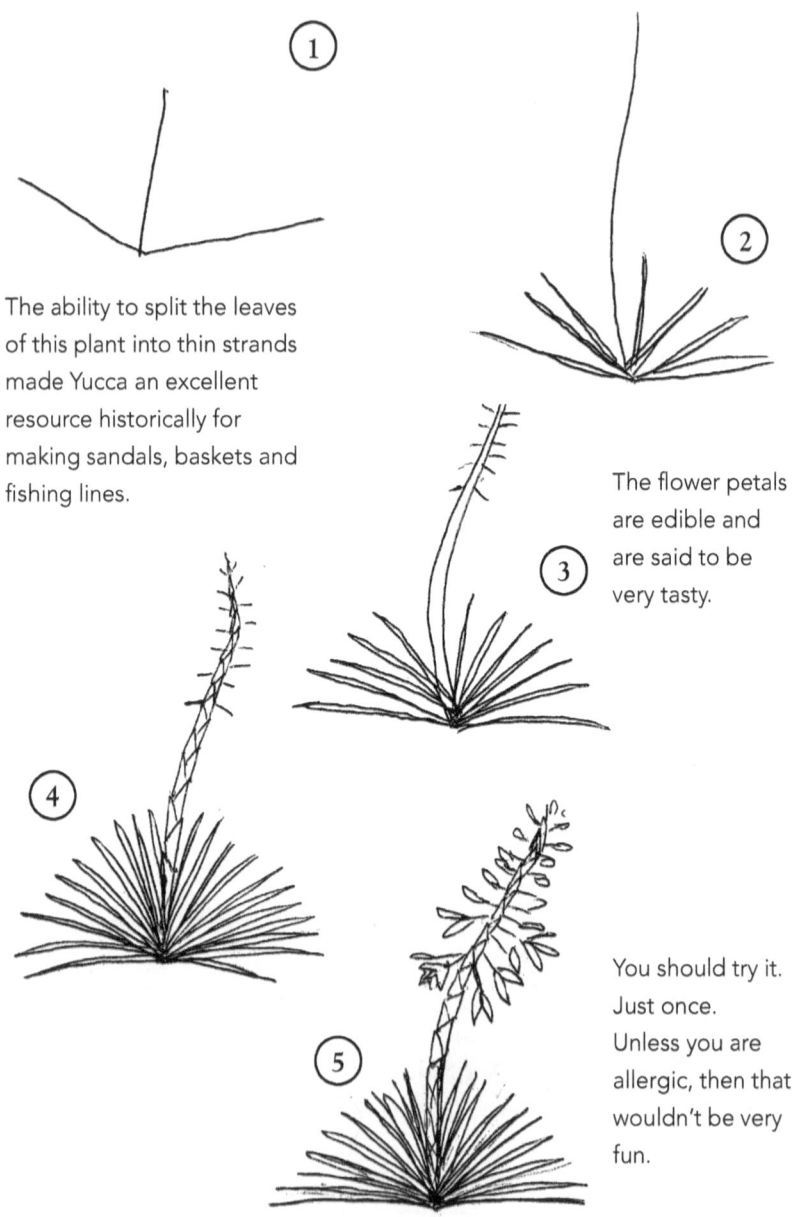

The ability to split the leaves of this plant into thin strands made Yucca an excellent resource historically for making sandals, baskets and fishing lines.

The flower petals are edible and are said to be very tasty.

You should try it. Just once. Unless you are allergic, then that wouldn't be very fun.

Elderberry
(Sambucus spp.)

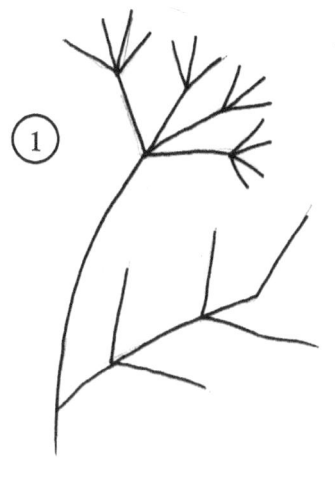

(1)

The Elderberry shrub has much to offer:

(2)

Its yellow and white flowers can be dried and steeped into a tea.

*See page 90

(3)

Its ripened berries, rich in vitamins, can be turned into jelly.

(4)

Yarrow
(Achillea millefolium)

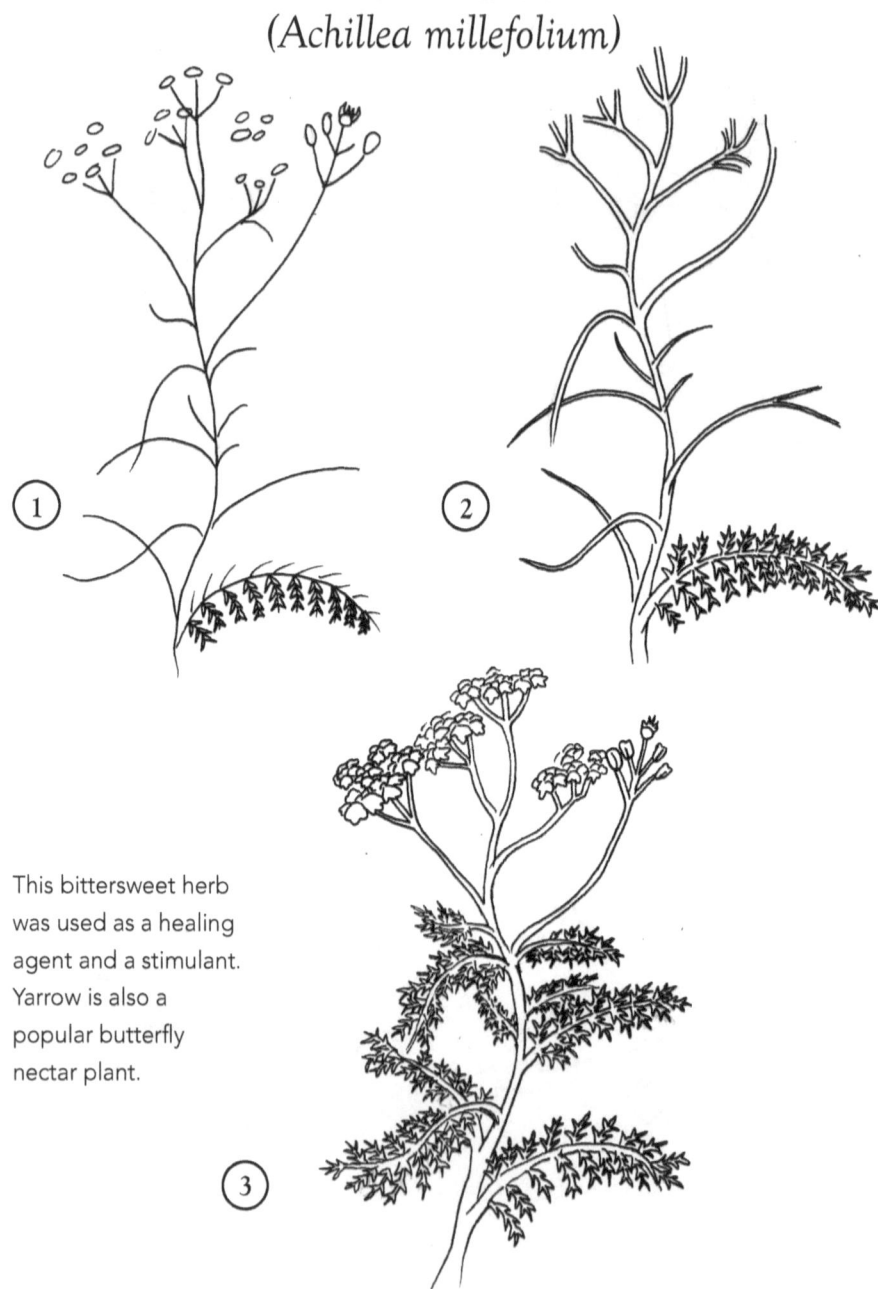

This bittersweet herb was used as a healing agent and a stimulant. Yarrow is also a popular butterfly nectar plant.

© Sama Wareh www.warehart.com

Poison Oak
(*Toxicodendron diversilobum*)

Not sure how to spot poison oak? Just remember this simple rhyme:

Leaves of three, let it be.
Unless it's hairy, then it's berry.

Sequoia Tree
(*Sequoia sempervirens*)

These are California's proudest trees, being the world's largest in terms of volume. The oldest Sequoia tree on record is 3,500 years old.

White Sage
(Salvia apiana)

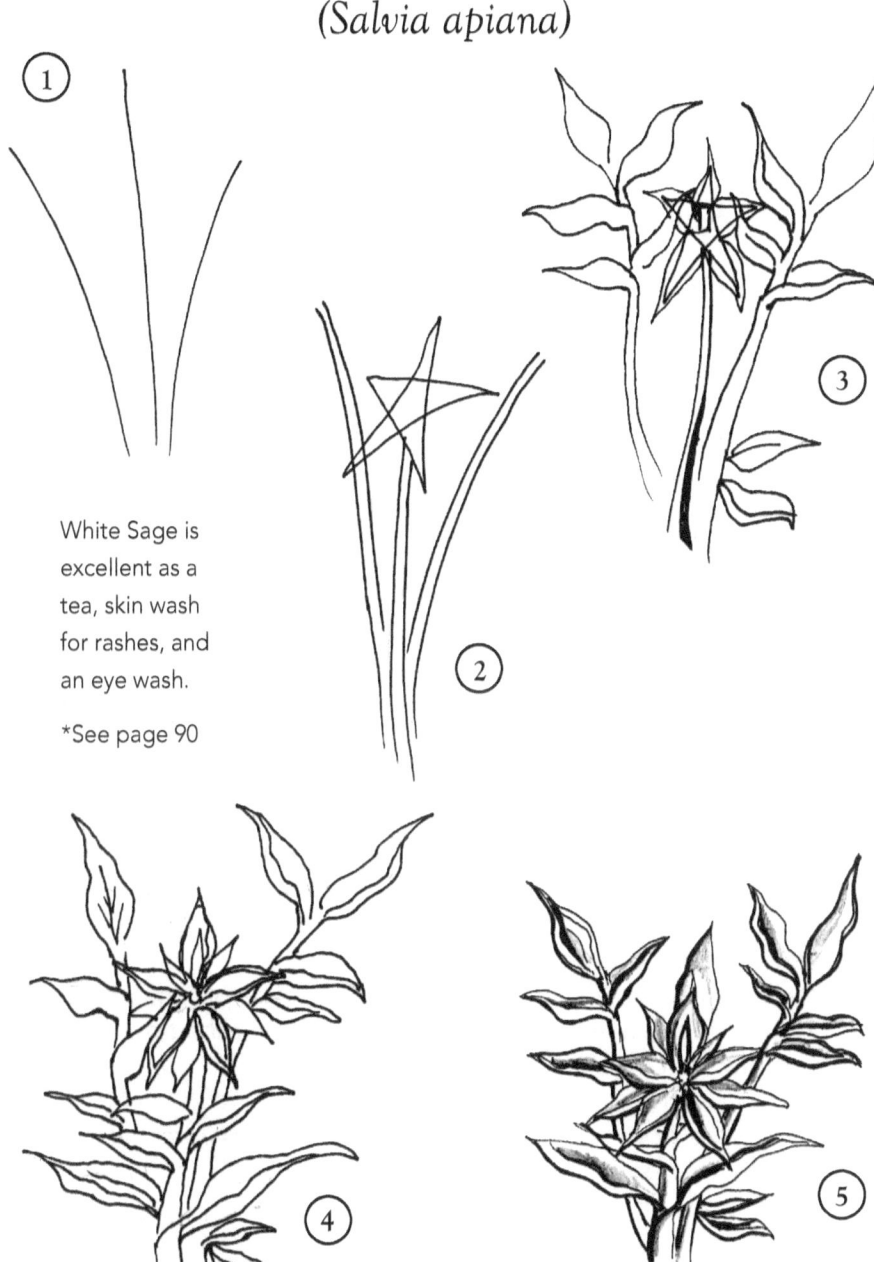

White Sage is excellent as a tea, skin wash for rashes, and an eye wash.

*See page 90

Plant Uses

There are various homeopathic plants around us that can be utilized as remedies in forms such as tonics, poultices and oils. Some can be used fresh, right there on the spot, like the prickly pear cactus. Others need a little preparation. All of the plants listed here definitely have something in common. While some may have more uses than others, they all make a great tea. Once dried, make sure to store in labelled air-tight glass jars for a lasting shelf life.

Just follow these simple steps, put on your favorite music and stick your little pinkie finger out while sipping tea properly from a teacup. Enjoy!

Black Sage
(Salvia mellifera)

Black Sage contains diterpenoids, which are pain relievers. It is excellent for fevers and helps with digestion. You may also apply cold tea to area of pain on body.

Pick, wash, and dry its leaves in the sun for a few weeks. You can tell when the leaves curl up a bit that they are ready for storing. Black Sage tea is very strong, so only use 3-5 leaves per teapot.

Buckwheat
(Eriogonum fasciculatum)

Depending on which part of this plant you use, you will get different remedies. If you use the stem as the base for the tea, it makes a great gargle remedy for bladder problems. Once the Buckwheat flowers dry, the seeds become a coarse grain, which can be ground and used as a flour or roasted as a base for tea. It is said that the flower seeds are good to fight type II Diabetes.

1. Pick the flowers when they are dry and separate the grains from the rest of the flower.
2. Rinse the buckwheat grain.
3. Let it sit and dry on a paper towel.
4. Place in a pan and roast on low heat.

Elderberry
(Sambucus nigra)

If you are considering making Buckwheat pancakes, Elderberry jam would be a nice topping to sweeten things up. When preparing Elderberry for tea, avoid using the stems, leaves and unripe berries, as they are poisonous. The infused flowers make an excellent decongestant.

1. Pick the yellow flowers off of the Elderberry plant.
2. Dry them on a towel. The drying process could take anywhere from one to two weeks depending on humidity.

Wild Rose
(Rosa californica)

The neat thing about Wild Rose is how all around beautiful it is. This beautiful yet medicinally beneficial plant is drought-tolerant and incredibly fragrant. Indigenous families made tea from the roots as a cold remedy.

The rose hips can survive winter, and will bring wildlife to your yard even during the wintertime. Rose hips are just a fancy phrase for delicious berries with high vitamin C content.

To make a tasty tea, dry the rose hips and the flowers and infuse with hot water.

White Sage
(Salvia apiana)

White Sage tea can fight congestion and help to decrease sweating and salivation.

1. Pick the leaves, wash them, and dry them for an easy tea. White Sage is very strong so be sure to only use a few leaves for an entire teapot.
2. For an eyewash, use cooled-down White Sage tea. It works!
3. For rashes, apply cold tea to itchy area.

How to Make a Journal from Cardboard

What you will need:
- ◊ Cutting tool (X-ACTO knife or box cutter)
- ◊ Ruler
- ◊ Duct tape
- ◊ Magazine cutouts (this will be used for covering your journal, so find pictures and/or text that you like)
- ◊ Glue
- ◊ Clear shipping tape or self laminating sheets
- ◊ Yarn
- ◊ Stone or seashell
- ◊ White computer paper cut in half (4.25" x 5.5")
- ◊ 2 binder clips
- ◊ ...and, of course, cardboard

Directions

1 Use cutting tool to trim cardboard to approximately 9" x 17" and lay it horizontally.

2 Along the top edge, measure 5" from each side and mark it. Repeat on bottom edge.

3 Place ruler between the top and bottom markings on left side, and score a vertical line, being careful not to slash all the way through the cardboard.
Repeat on right side

This should allow the cardboard to fold.

Now that you have the skeleton structure of your outdoor sketchpad, a little creativity is in order.

4 Cover all edges with duct tape.

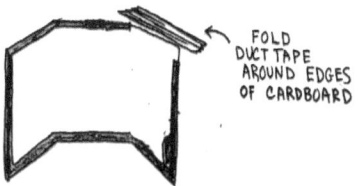

FOLD DUCT TAPE AROUND EDGES OF CARDBOARD

5 Glue magazine cutouts to cover the entire outer shell. For durability, use clear shipping tape or self-laminating sheets to cover the magazine strips you have affixed to the cover. You can even cover the entire journal with it! This will protect your journal from rain and also from falling apart.

6 With cutting tool, poke two holes on either side of folding journal.

7 Cut a piece of yarn long enough to wrap around the journal (while closed). Thread yarn through the two holes and tie a knot so that you are left with one long string on the outside of the journal.

8 On the inside of the journal, add a strip of magazine paper that has been reinforced with tape on both sides and tape it so it straddles the crease. This will be the pen holder for your journal.

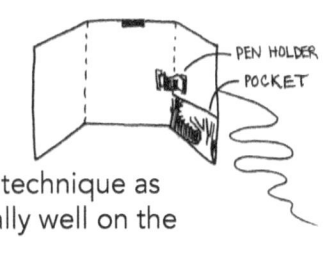

PEN HOLDER
POCKET

9 Create any pockets using the same technique as the pen holder strip. Pockets do really well on the inside of your journal.

10 Close the journal and affix a small stone or seashell to one side so that the yarn can wrap around it.

11 It's best to find something that has an outwardly conical shape so that the yarn can wrap itself around and under.

12 Attach the 4.25" x 5.5" computer paper to the middle inside of journal with a binder clip.

HOW TO DRAW HANDOUT
4.25" x 5.5"

DRAWING PAPER
4.25" x 5.5"

13 With another binder clip, attach photocopied handouts from "How to Draw Series" onto right or left side of journal cover.

14 Attach another pen holder magazine strip to front cover.

15 For field sketching with a letter sized sheet, turn the journal vertically and move the clip to the top. Remove all the other papers and you have a handy outdoor clipboard!

Index

About the Author

Sama Wareh holds a Master's of Science degree in Environmental Education and Communication from California State University Fullerton and a Bachelors Degree in Filmmaking and Art. During her eight years in the Environmental Education field, Sama has led hundreds of hikes, designed curriculum for hands-on environmental education programs, and has taught Art, Social Science, and Physical Science to adults, scouts, students, teachers, and the general public. She has been invited as a guest lecturer and workshop presenter at many universities, churches, and institutes, with her main focus on conservation, water issues, and seeing nature through art.

Sama has participated in art shows in venues all over the country (including the Bowers Museum and the Zeitgeist Multicultural Institute in New Orleans), has illustrated children's books, and has sold art internationally for over ten years. Moved and constantly in awe of the diversity of nature and people, Sama's thirst for knowledge and acquaintance with the unknown has driven her on many backpacking adventures, from filming landscapes in the Mediterranean hills of Syria to walking jaguars in the deep wild jungles of Bolivia. Sama lives life as a form of art, adding a constant stream of inspiration to her work.

In 2013, Sama was awarded OC Register's OCMetro, 40 under 40 award.

To contact Sama or view her artwork,
please visit www.warehart.com